DAD DUTY
Seattle

*dad-tested kid-approved adventures
that won't bore your socks off*

Copyright © 2005 DadDuty.com

10-Digit ISBN 1-59113-840-X
13-Digit ISBN 978-1-59113-840-2

All rights reserved. No part of this publication may be reproduced, stored in a retrieval system, or transmitted in any form or by any means, electronic, mechanical, recording or otherwise, without the prior written permission of the author. To contact the author email info@DadDuty.com or visit http://www.DadDuty.com.

The editorial comments in this publication are the sole opinion of the author. No fees or services were rendered in exchange for inclusion in this publication. While every effort was made to ensure the accuracy of the information, details are subject to change and the publisher and author assume no responsibility for errors or omissions, or for damages resulting from the use of the information contained herein.

All trademarks and registered trademarks remain the property of their respective owners. Where those designations appear in this book and the author was aware of a trademark claim, the designations have been printed in initial caps.

Printed in the United States of America.

Published by Booklocker.com, Inc.
2005

DAD DUTY
Seattle

*dad-tested kid-approved adventures
that won't bore your socks off*

A HANDBOOK FOR DADS,
BY EAN VENT

~ Booklocker.com ~

Dedicated to the J-man and the Ab-ster

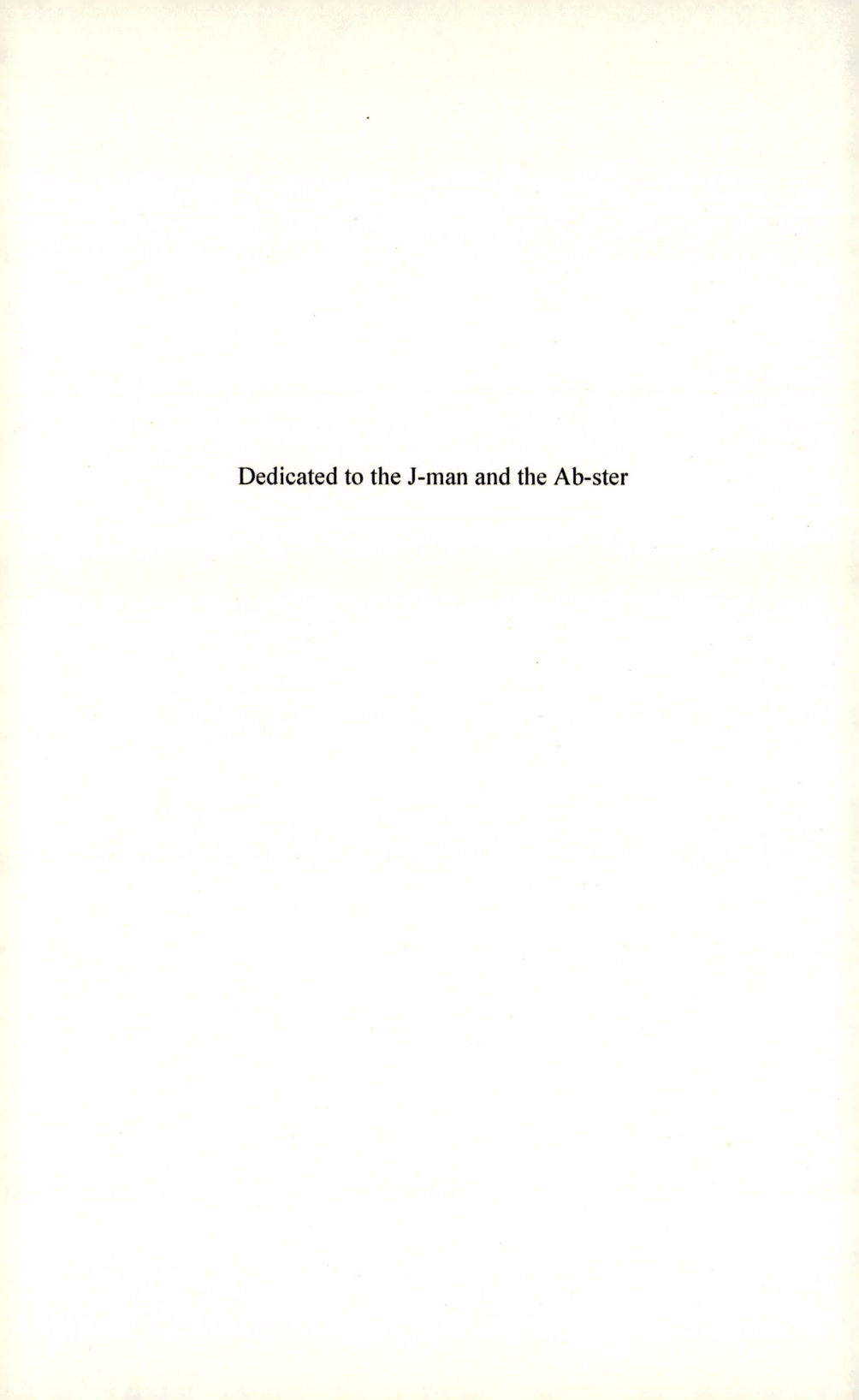

Contents

Forward	IX
Introduction	XIII
1. Downtown	1
2. Visualize Ballard	7
3. Dump Run	13
4. Green Lake Anytime	17
5. Ferry Escape	21
6. Pipes, Pipes…Greenwood Car Show	25
7. The Need For Speed - Evergreen Speedway	29
8. Seafair – Blue Angels & Hydros	33
9. Snoqualmie Calls	39
10. Alki Beach Day	43
11. Remlinger Farms	47
12. Take Me Out to the… Ballgame	51
13. Emerald Ups & Downs	55
14. Funtasia Daze Ya	59
15. Making Tracks at Traxx	63
16. Pacific Raceways Extravaganza	67
Dad Duty Cheat Sheet	71
Bench Warmers	73
That's a Wrap	79
About the Author	81
Acknowledgments	83

"Adventure is worthwhile in itself."
–Amelia Earhart

Forward

So you're on Dad Duty, what are you going to do now? And, if you're never on *duty*, you better start now **Dad**, and give those ladies a break! As a dad, you hold the unique ability to pull off adventures that kids love, and moms would rather avoid. The youngsters really do grow fast, and this remains your chance to shine. Discover what to do in Seattle when you're on duty, and what not to do.

Why do the other guide books *highly* recommend the Pike Place Market, the Experience Music Project, and the Pioneer Square Underground Tour? Sure, these outings sound good on paper, but when young kids enter the equation, disaster looms at every turn.

Why not go to Pike Place Market? If you wonder why your kid throws a tantrum in the middle of the market while you eye large veggies and sample garlic jelly, here's a clue for you: "a sea of knee caps is not that interesting when you are 2½ feet tall!" However, if you're prepared to buy a king salmon, watch it sail through the air, kiss the golden pig, and head to the beach to BBQ your prize, then this book is for you!

But why not experience the Music Project? Wait until you dish out beaucoup bucks for your surround sound headphones with high hopes for a musical escape, and then your kids quickly tire of banging on instruments after three minutes. You won't be enjoying audio bites on the skater punk era for long when they disperse in all directions laughing, yelling and crying.

Underground Tour? Perhaps you'll heed the other guide's recommendations and take your kids to the underground hazard in Pioneer Square. You'll score a few points laughing at Mr. Crapper's toilet jokes, but wait until you're the only idiot in the catacomb with a crying child – that place echoes like a concert hall.

No sir, this is not another *excellently prepared* but *useless* guide with 428 overwhelmingly wonderful things to do (with entire chapters on "how to prepare your kids for the art museum"). If you want to cut to the chase and find dad-tested kid-approved outings for your Dad Duty, then read on soldier...

"The ultimate measure of a man is not where he stands in moments of comfort, but where he stands at times of challenge and controversy."
–Martin Luther King, Jr.

INTRODUCTION

Each outing in this book was meticulously crafted and tuned for maximum applicability in seven key categories. Comprehensive mathematical models evaluate each aspect of the adventure at hand and culminate into a multi-faceted rating scale known as: the Bore-o-Meter (bōr-ŏm'ĭ-tər). For Vent knows, a *bored* dad quickly becomes an irritable dad, and an irritable dad ain't gonna have much patience! Alas, without patience, all is lost.

Simply focus on the seven key ingredients for Dad-Duty success:

Movement – anything moving qualifies. Extreme speed is best, but general rocking motion is acceptable.

Machinery – self explanatory. Anything mechanical is a crowd pleaser.

Loudness – fear and awe generally accompany loud sound. This is good.

Largeness – something about larger-than-life really inspires.

Food – sustenance is a necessity on any adventure. Diets and nutrition? Do your best but there's always tomorrow.

Sugar – all outings require sweets on some order. Even a few lollipops in a pocket will do wonders.

Rhythm – probably the most underrated aspect of Dad Duty, here's your secret sauce for success. Never let a good thing go south by dragging it out. Keep on the go, Joe.

Each category averages into the final Bore-o-Meter score. The higher the rating out of 5.0, the greater the chance you'll chalk up some lasting memories. For example, say you get snookered into going to the Seattle
Children's Museum. No worries, the Dad Duty Bore-o-Meter will nix this trip before you begin. Anything under a 3.5 forget it – and the Children's Museum only measures a dismal 2.0 on the Bore-o-Meter:

Seattle Children's Museum:

Movement	■□□□□
Machinery	■□□□□
Loudness	■■■□□
Largeness	■□□□□
Food	■■■□□
Sugar	■■■□□
Rhythm	■■□□□

Bore-o-Meter: 2.0

Here's how it goes: you arrive at the museum with a backpack full of miscellanea depending on the age of your kids (wipies, diapers, pull-ups, sippy-cups, binkies, onesies, fishies, and maybe even a few bottles of freshly pumped breast milk). Luckily, you also stuffed your pockets with sweets from a distant Halloween for the inevitable emergency. At the museum, the attractions mildly entertain your kids, even though this is their 22nd time (or soon will be), but you're terminally bored. At least you can look around at the other bozos sitting on benches watching the clock.

The Bore-o-Meter knows better: low awe factor with the various museum gadgetry and play things, so Movement and Machinery suffer. Loudness registers a 3.0 but it's the annoying head-ache inducing kind. Fortunately, the sweets you brought bumped up the Sugar rating, and upstairs the food court serves good eats. All in all, a no-go 2 point 0.

> **VENTS VENTS** "Any destination ending in rium or seum must strictly be avoided!"

As Vent says, avoid the *riums* and *seums* such as aquarium, planetarium, museum, auditorium...ad nauseum! Save these outings for the in-laws and school fieldtrips. Don't worry, your kids will get cultured, but you can concentrate on adventures that knock your kids' socks off – or, at least get something useful done like a trip to the dump. Now, let's go...

> **VENTS VENTS** "The only guide book recommending the town dump as a top attraction!"

✴ READER TIPS

The bulk of this book highlights the Seattle outings that make the Bore-o-Meter cut (the best of which contain heavy doses of testosterone and loud noise). Each outing tells dads where to go, and how to keep up the rhythm to avoid boredom. Simple maps get you to the destination with no fuss, and *Vent's Vents* keep you out of trouble along the way.

In addition, the *Bench Warmers* section provides other ideas that especially help new dads. These bench warmers did not make the starting line up, but they'll score a few points for you.

Finally, for those readers who can't help peeking at the end of the book first, don't miss the *Cheat Sheet*. The *Cheat Sheet* provides a quick way to evaluate all the outings based on time available and driving distance. When the tantrums start to take over, just consult the cheat sheet and head out the door.

✷Also check out http://www.DadDuty.com, the official Dad Duty website operated by Ean Vent. Find more info and web links for each outing, join the forums to share your own success stories (and dramatic failures) and meet other dads online.

1. DOWNTOWN

Surviving downtown with kids can daunt even the savviest Seattle dad. Perhaps you can still survive the Pioneer Square bar-crawl without peril, but now you must parallel park a mini-van full of screaming toddlers in a traffic jam! But Vent's got the trick to maintain sanity: public transportation. Yes, the keys to the city and Bore-o-Meter success lie on the Monorail, the Bus Tunnel, and the Trolley cars. All three connect beautifully for cheap, convenient transportation. Park once, and navigate the entire city with ease: Seattle Center, Westlake Center, Pioneer Square, International District, and the Waterfront.

Movement	■■■■■
Machinery	■■■■■
Loudness	■■■■☐
Largeness	■■■■☐
Food	■■■■■
Sugar	■■■■■
Rhythm	■■■■■

Bore-o-Meter: 4.7

High on the Movement and Machinery scale, as well as Loudness and Largeness, you can keep up the Rhythm by jumping from place to place. The monorail connects Seattle Center to Westlake Center. The bus tunnel from Westlake connects to terminals at Pioneer Square and the International District. And the trolley cars connect to the Waterfront Piers. You'll cover lots of terrain and avoid several mus*eums* in the process. Park at any leg of the journey and then improvise based on time.

At Seattle Center, the kids love the carnival scene right next to the Space Needle. Buy some tickets and ride the kiddy-spaceships, the rollercoaster, and the Ferris wheel. But be sure you bought all your tickets before attempting the milk-jug throw. At $5.00 for 6 throws, those darn jugs quickly drain a wallet. If you actually knock all three bottles over please drop an email to Jugs@DadDuty.com.

Next, jump the Monorail that connects Seattle Center to Westlake Center. For only a few bucks fare you'll pass by the funky Experience Music Project building (that supposedly looks like a guitar?) and wind by the shiny sky scrapers. If you sit in the front next to the driver, you'll find the best views and excitement. A short ride, but great food awaits you at Westlake Center. Grab some eats, take a seat, and watch the passing monorail while you feast. Then, if time is short, head back to Seattle Center on the Monorail; otherwise, your goal lies ahead at Pioneer Square via the bus.

The highest kid-rating in downtown goes to the bus tunnel. It departs directly from the bowels of Westlake center and connects beautifully to your next stop at Pioneer Square. Plus, kids love the ominous circular tubes ready to transport them into the unknown. Lightly advertised, and lightly used, the tunnel cuts right through the heart of the city. Clean, cool architecture, and FREE – don't knock it until you've tried it.

Unfortunately, (and ironically, given the bus tunnel light-rail controversy in the 90's) you may have to wait. The tunnel is closed from September 2005 until 2007 for track refitting. During this period, dads are forced to attempt the more seedy surface routes. But lots of routes traverse downtown on 1st through 5th Street, so head out and wing it, or get organized and use the convenient King county *trip planner* at http://transit.metrokc.gov. You can always check out *www.DadDuty.com* for the latest recommendations and navigation tips from other dads.

If the tunnel is open, you're in luck: just ride the escalators from the food court down, down, and then down some more to the tunnel entrance. Take the South bus and be sure to skip the University Station (unless you're a masochist shopper) and depart at Pioneer Square.

At Pioneer Square you'll find the Smith Tower, the Occidental Park eateries, and the George Benson Waterfront Trolley connection. And, unless you have an infant or toddler along, you can take the Seattle Underground Tour. Otherwise Vent's law states that a tantrum will happen at the worst possible moment while under the city.

✻If the Smith Tower viewing deck is open, go for it. It's a bit pricy, but totally worth it in half-decent weather. The innocuous Smith Tower entrance is on the corner of 2nd and Yesler Way. Step inside and greet the elevator man for a ride to the 35th floor in a funky old-fashioned elevator (circa 1914). Exit into the ornate Chinese Room and head outside for surround-Sound views. The experience from atop the Smith Tower wrap-around balcony can permanently etch itself in toddler-memory. Thereafter, every time you drive by downtown, the triangle tower marks your outing by day, and the big blue light marks it by night.

Next, from Pioneer Square, your adventure can continue on the Trolley to the Waterfront. Kids love the trolley; however, if you started at Seattle Center, you're creating quite a back-trail. It has been done, but be ready for very tired troops. The piers offer good views, food, IMAX, and a tucked away carousel.

Or, from Pioneer Square, take the bus tunnel to the International District. Don't forget to get off the bus, or you'll find yourself at the airport! Let the kids run around a bit in the courtyard and play on the smooth rocks surrounding the fountain near the tunnel entrance. Across the street, Uwajimaya provides a convenient bathroom stop and more great eats. Mostly, you're just turning around at this stop. Retrace your steps back to Westlake, up the escalators to the Monorail, and finish off at Seattle Center with more carnival rides and cotton candy. Whew!

✻Food options abound at every stop: the Seattle Center food court above the Children's Museum, the Westlake Center food court (Vent's Pick), the Uwajimaya food court in the International District, the local Pioneer Square eateries, and the Waterfront seafood restaurants. This doesn't even mention all the great restaurants that scatter the entire city – eating won't be a problem.

✻A great wading pool sits adjacent to the north end of the Key Arena with cool fountains, climbing rocks, and remains mostly unknown.

✻Ride The Ducks also departs from Seattle Center. See the Bench Warmers section for this fun tip and bus & boat around town.

Dad Duty Seattle

GETTING AROUND DOWNTOWN

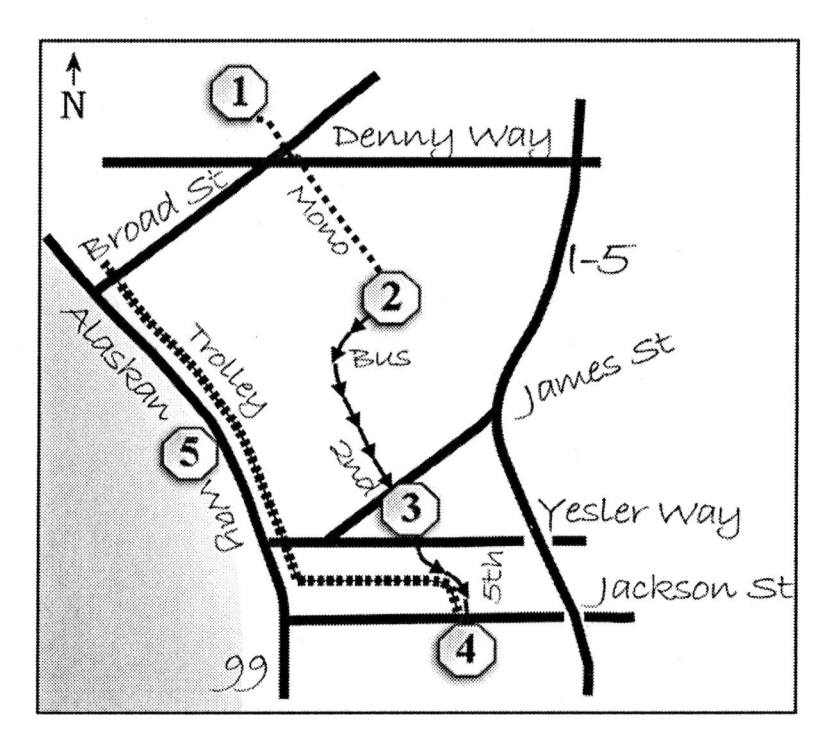

1. **Seattle Center** – http://www.seattlemonorail.com (206) 905-2600
2. **Westlake Center** – Food court, Monorail, Bus Tunnel (*400 Pine St.*)
3. **Pioneer Square** – Smith Tower, Trolley cars, Bus tunnel station
4. **International District** – Uwajimaya food court, Bus tunnel station
5. **Waterfront Piers** – Trolley cars, Imax, Eateries, Boat tours

✶ visit http://transit.metrokc.gov/ for trolley and bus route info and maps

2. Visualize Ballard

Try out Ballard for a sea-themed adventure packed with boats galore, fishing paraphernalia, spawning salmon, and soft beach sand. Hit the docks, then the locks, and finish off with a view of the Puget Sound at the beach. While less thrilling than the Blue Angels or Mariner baseball at Safeco, you can "Visualize Ballard" anytime and earn kid points.

Movement	■■■■☐
Machinery	■■■■☐
Loudness	■■■☐☐
Largeness	■■■■■
Food	■■■☐☐
Sugar	■■■■■
Rhythm	■■■■☐

Bore-o-Meter: 4.28

Located just southwest of the Ballard Bridge, there's always something going on at the docks of the Fisherman's Terminal. Just park, and walk out any random dock to enjoy the rusty cacophony of oil, metal, fish, and sea. Here you'll find the North Pacific commercial fishing fleet, and the heart and soul of Ballard's Scandinavian roots. Some vessels seem barely sea worthy, as if they first sailed in 1917 when the locks were built. Others fill the gamut from clunky, funky, utilitarian, mysterious, and shiny new. Kids enjoy checking out the miscellaneous trolling gear and reading the wild boat names. Try to strike up a conversation with a leathered fisherman and see how the catch is going or what season is on.

Ean Vent

Once you tire of the docks, hit the Locks. Travel back over the Ballard Bridge and then west through downtown Ballard. The officially named Hiram M. Chittenden Locks really tip the Bore-o-Meter scales for Movement and Machinery. Always transporting cool yachts and sailboat traffic, often you'll see a giant fishery boat, a tug boat, or the coast guard passing through. No matter what, the Locks entertain the kids (for a while), especially when a yachtsman slips off his port side into the drink, or a passing patrol boat brags that they just pulled a hypothermic sail-boater out of the Sound. To boot, during spawning season the steelhead and salmon leap upstream in packs, and fly out of the water with big splash effects.

VENTS/STNƎΛ   There's no greater buzz kill than trekking over to an empty fish ladder

As Vent says, make sure it's salmon season before you trek over the dam to the glass viewing chamber. When it's salmon season you'll see some giant kings and steelheads milling about. June-September's a good bet and you can also check daily fish counts online or just ask a dock worker.

If you're extremely lucky, you'll experience a sea lion that ignored the orca sound protection in the channel, and mercilessly preys on the schooling salmon. The fish swarm back and forth hundreds at a time, but with nowhere to run they easily fall victim to the speedy sea lion. The crowd loves it, but the fish wardens would rather transport that sea lion to Alcatraz, literally. One pesky sea lion was bagged-and-tagged and dropped off in San Diego, only to show up a few weeks later for an easy meal. No kidding.

✲Please support your local vendors and purchase lots of popsicles and ice-cream bars from the treat trailer next to the Lock's entrance gate. Parking is no longer free and as a result, business has drooped. Why? The city bought the land from the train folks and rewarded us with brand new meters.

When the Locks are beat, grab a treat and head for the beach. If you forgot cash for the treat trailer outside the Locks entrance, just drive northwest around the point past Shilshole Bay Marina until you find the Little Coney diner. They take credit cards, and offer great fried fare. Don't skimp on the obligatory soft-serve twist cones to bump up the Bore-o-Meter Sugar category.

A click further and you will dead end into Golden Gardens Park. The northern sand is best, as far away from the fire pits as possible to avoid charcoal covered feet. Check out the sailboaters and kiteboarders framed by the Olympics (when exposed), skip some rocks into the water, and let the sand do the rest. There's also a swath of grass at the northernmost parking area for tag, football, and frolicking. Golden Gardens wins anytime the Seattle sun peaks out.

Ean Vent

✴Dog owners may enjoy the dog park up the hill a bit from Golden Gardens on Seaview Pl NW. You can walk up from the park through the forest, or drive and park in the lot. Let the pups foray a bit while you enjoy the forest atmosphere.

✴Even if you don't have a dog along, a walk through the old-growth offers a mini-adventure unto itself. From the entrance of the Golden Gardens northern parking lot (just in front of the kids play structure), take the tunnel under the railroad tracks. This drops out into another parking area where you must walk up Seaview Place a hundred yards until you find a set of stairs. Keep on trucking up the stairs to the dog area and bathrooms. Wander the trails throughout the area, and if you cross the road, you can conquer the trail all the way to the top. You'll finish with a last agonizing set of stairs and find yourself at the corner of 85th and 32nd. As a reward, drinks and espresso await across the street at Café Fiore.

GETTING AROUND BALLARD

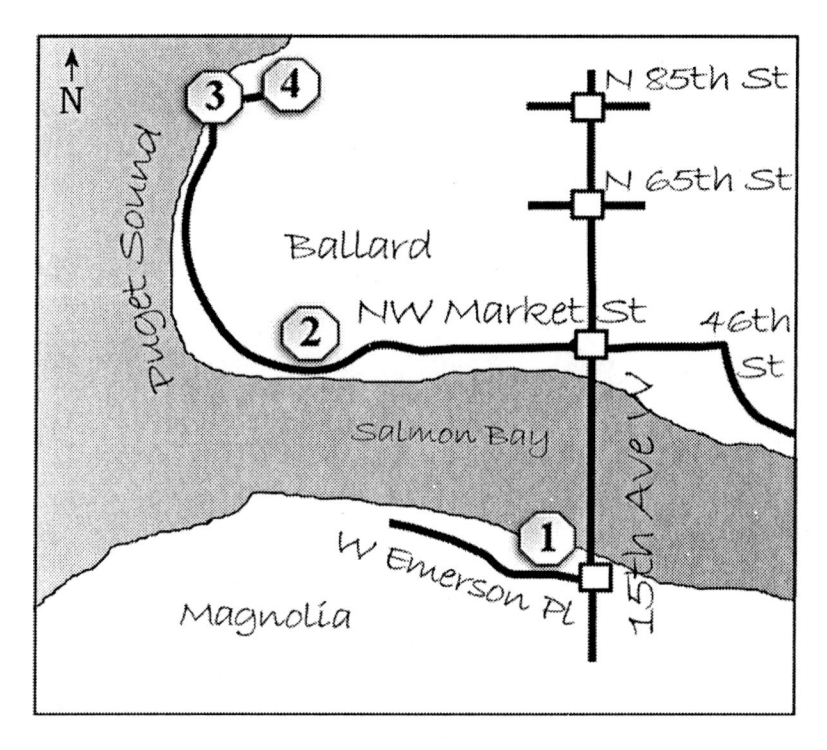

1. **Fisherman's Terminal** –free parking in lots, walk to docks
   http://www.nwseaport.org (206) 447-9800
2. **Locks** – NW 54th St and 32nd Ave NW, pay to park
   http://www.nws.usace.army.mil (206) 764-3742
3. **Golden Gardens** - 54th St turns into Seaview Ave NW
4. **Café Fiore** – NW 85th St and 32nd Ave NW (up the hill)

VENTS

Never hit the dump
without a kid in tow...

3. Dump Run

Who would've guessed that the North Seattle Dump on 34th and Stone Way would rate so high for kid enjoyment and repeatability. Never hit the dump without a kid in tow, because not only do piles of junk interest kids in general, the experience lasts a life time. Picture truckloads of people hucking trash into a giant heap while a menacing caged bull dozer crams the debris into a gaping metal hole, along with coverall clad men in gasmasks who douse the pile with fire hoses and create a thick cloud of dusty mist that permeates the reeking air – it doesn't get much better!

Movement	■■■■■
Machinery	■■■■■
Loudness	■■■■■
Largeness	■■■■■
Food	■■■■■
Sugar	■■■□□
Rhythm	■■■■■

Bore-o-Meter: 4.7

Fortuitously, the dump lies in close proximity to the Northlake Tavern where you can score a giant pizza. It also sits close to Gas Works Park so grab some balls, bats, and blankets before you depart. Put this triple combo together (the dump, a pizza, and a park) and the Bore-o-Meter starts to sizzle. If only someone would open an ice cream parlor on Stone Way it would register a perfect 5.0; however the local 7-11 will have to do.

✶The dump line does back up, so grab snacks *before* you get stuck in the dump line with bored kids. Hopefully, a ballgame will be on while you wait, otherwise it's acceptable to roll down the windows and blast country music.

Ean Vent

Just before you dump your load, order a Northlake Tavern pizza at 206-633-5317. Known to locals as the biggest, greasiest, and tastiest pie in all of Seattle, this pile of cheese won't disappoint. They slow cook your pizza for at least 30 minutes, so time your takeout call appropriately. Twenty-one and older only inside the tavern, so you'll be on the takeout plan. Then double back and take your prize to Gas Works Park for the feast.

With the Food category pegged, all the left over pipery at Gasworks Park will bump your Machinery category even higher. Enjoy the downtown views across the water, the float planes overhead, and the green grass underfoot. Also, the Burke-Gilman bike trail departs from the Gas Works parking lot if you brought the bikes. This trail is pretty busy, so Vent recommends keeping the beginners off the slopes.

VENTS VENTS
What do you need a guide book for when a kite and green grass do wonders?

✷To top off your outing with a fun tidbit, drop by the troll under the Aurora Bridge. Every kid deserves to experience the giant troll grabbing the VW at least once or twice – it's a Seattle icon. The troll lives under the bridge on N. 36th St and Aurora Ave N, just north of downtown Freemont. For a special treat, drop by the troll for "Trollaween" on the night of October 31st. Wander the streets in your Halloween garb with the fire-puppets and unique Freemont locals.

✷Another fun diversion: take the kids to Agua Verde for a kayak ride! Only a few blocks further East from Northlake Tavern on Boat Street you can rent a two or three seater and tool around the channel. Agua Verde is also directly off the Burke-Gilman bike trail if you want to attempt a bike-kayak combo.
http://www.aguaverde.com (206) 545-8570

DUMP DUTY

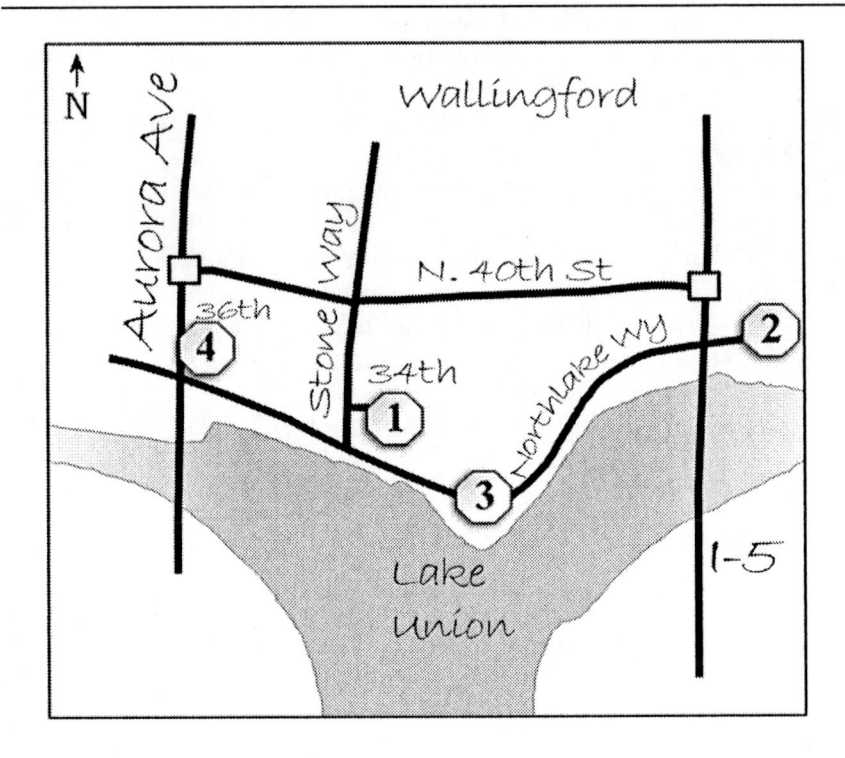

1. **North Recycling and Disposal Station** – 1350 North 34th Street
2. **Northlake Tavern** – 660 N.E. Northlake Way (206) 633-5317
3. **Gas Works Park** – 2101 N Northlake Way
4. **Aurora Bridge Troll** – N 36th Street and Aurora Place North

4. GREEN LAKE ANYTIME

Green Lake thrives year round with dog walkers, bikers, trikers, trendy joggers, and the occasional moron in a Speedo. Lots of sights and sounds stimulate the kids, with plenty of room to run and tire themselves out. Especially attractive for its central location, grass, playground, and plenty of restaurants, Green Lake saves the day anytime for the unplanned Dad Duty.

Movement	■■■■□
Machinery	■■■□□
Loudness	■■■□□
Largeness	■■■□□
Food	■■■■■
Sugar	■■■■■
Rhythm	■■■■□

Bore-o-Meter: 3.85

Warning: you may encounter a healthy dose of hot women, so keep your focus on the job (you're a Dad now anyway dude) or one kid will be teetering off a dock while the other heads across the busy road to check out the rabbits! If you didn't know already, Green Lake ranks pretty high on the yuppie dating scene.

If your kids are stroller bound, you're set. Just hit the trail until things fall apart and then go to the playground. Otherwise, drag along the bikes, boards, and blades and let 'em ride. Don't tick off the locals and block the entire path with strollers and bikes – pay attention to wheels on one side and walkers on the other. You may create a disaster when a biker or rollerblader blasts around a corner to meet your wall of strollers. But don't get too anal about it; some crabby walkers go a little overboard. Plus, that wannabe speed skater with one arm behind his back ought to slow down anyway.

Ean Vent

The Food and Sugar categories bump this outing over the 3.5 Bore-o-Meter bar no problem. You'll find great kid-friendly eats in any of the clusters around the north and east sides of the lake. The toughest part is choosing where to eat; but regardless, you must stop at the Mix for ice cream and toppings mixed on the marble-top. This remains mandatory!

To the North, across the street from the wading pool area, you will find World Wraps, Zeek's Pizza, and the Mix ice cream shop. Zeek's serves slices, has a television inside typically tuned to sporting events, and also serves micro-brews (obviously a top choice for Vent). To the east, Rosita's Mexican restaurant is on Woodlawn (one block past Baskin Robbins at 7210 Woodlawn Ave). This is a sit down affair, but very kid friendly and loud enough to mask wild kids.

To the Southeast from the kid's playground, you'll find fried food or Mexican. Just walk across the playing fields and south of the Albertsons. Spuds serves up great fish-n-chips, and fried anything. Tacos Guamas offers more excellent Mexican food and a salsa bar. The cheesy bean burritos are a kid favorite. However, don't forget to swing back by the Mix.

Since this outing gears itself more towards the casual anytime outing, the Bore-o-Meter loses a few ticks in Machinery, Loudness, and Largeness. Every outing can't blow your mind, and in this case you'll replace the Loudness category with peaceful park noise, laughter, and random bits of conversations overhead on the path. All in all, it makes for a nice day.

✷If the nearby restaurants aren't enough for you, try Diggity Dogs for a real gem. The kids will dig the dogs, and you can score a spicy Andouille (Ahn-doo-ee) and load it with the works from the topping bar. Diggity Dogs is located up from the southeast end of the lake on the corner of 56th and Kenwood. Seasoned Green-Lakers will remember this corner from the Honey Bear Bakery glory days. Unfortunately, the local joggers, cyclists, and early risers who waited patiently in line for morning espresso and a whole-wheat cinnamon roll lost out; but TangleTown brewery moved in and saved the day with fresh Elysian microbrews. It's a moot point for dads since you won't be hitting TangleTown with the kids; but it's tough to beat Diggity Dogs: kid-friendly to the max, and dad can order a bottled beer.

VENTS SUNEA
What's with all the rabbits anyway?
They're procreating like...uh, rabbits.

✳ The rabbits live on the west side of the lake in the grassy areas where Whitman Pl N tunnels under Aurora Ave. With no natural predators, the population appears to be thriving.

✳ Check out the makeshift BMX jump course at the south Green Lake fields. You'll likely find soccer and baseball games in progress, more rabbits, and some BMX'ers jumping around on the hilly mounds. Easy kid entertainment.

✳ Green Lake Bonuses: crew boats, fishing derby, luminaries, wading pool, playground, game fields, BMX jump course, and the must-do Milk Carton Derby during Seafair (see the Bench Warmers section).

Ean Vent

GETTIN' AROUND GREEN LAKE

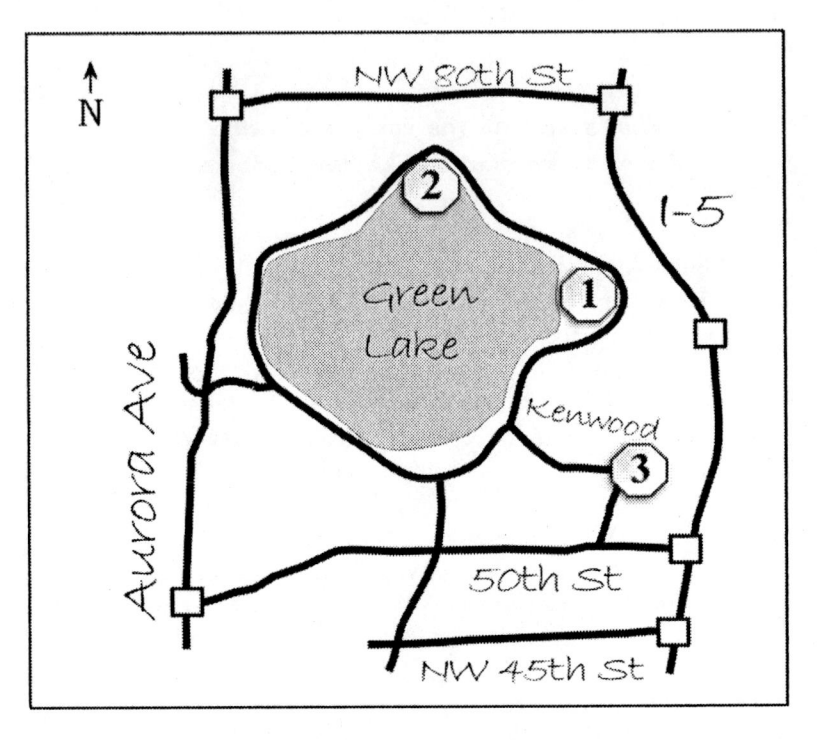

1. Playground, Fields, Tacos Guamas, Spuds, Albertsons
2. Wading Pool, World Wraps, Zeek's Pizza, Mix Ice Cream
3. Diggity Dogs (56th and Kenwood, or Meridian off of 50th St)

5. Ferry Escape

The ferry holds high kid-value simply because big boats are cool. Plus, the splendor of the Puget Sound itself can't be overlooked or overbooked. Three convenient boats leave right out of Downtown and get you rolling without much thinking or preparation. Each ferry moves quickly enough to avoid public transportation boredom: Bainbridge (only 35 minute crossing time), Vashon (also 35 minutes), and Bremerton (1 hour cross time). Kids love the aspect of driving onto and parking their car on a boat, or if the car lines are long, you can park and go on foot.

Movement	■■■■
Machinery	■■■■
Loudness	■■■□
Largeness	■■■□
Food	■■□□
Sugar	■■■□
Rhythm	■■□□

Bore-o-Meter: 4.0

The Bore-o-Meter loves the ferry outing just for the ride alone: Large, Loud, Moving Machinery that also carries Food and Sugary treats. Although the food fails to impress, it is fast, convenient, and junky. Make sure you keep up the Rhythm because inside the cabin gets stuffy quick. You don't want an outing replete with back bending tantrums – upon the slightest sign of unrest, ditch your booth and get outside. The chilly wind and the seagulls do wonders.

Vents' pick for best destination goes to Bremerton because it's the longest ride and the most scenic. Plus, it's the only destination where the town lies in walking distance; so if you're going on foot, Bremerton remains your best bet. But most importantly, the Bore-o-Meter loves

Bremerton because the Navy Destroyer *USS Turner Joy* is parked right next to the terminal!

The Bore-o-Meter jumps up several notches with Bremerton and the USS Turner Joy. Only a few paces from the Ferry exit, the two imposing 5 inch/54 caliber gun turrets stand ready to greet you. Also on deck of this 1960s era Forrest Sherman class Destroyer you'll find two Mark 32 torpedo launchers, one on the port and one on the starboard. One more 5 inch long-barrel in the bow and all weapon systems are a go! Inside, explore pretty much the entire ship via tiny doors and cool ladders connecting compartments. Head to the bridge, take the helm, sit in the captain's chair, inspect the engine room, and finish up by purchasing some maritime gadgetry at the ship store. All in all, it's a kick.

> "In life, it's not the destination that matters, it's the Ferry."

If your time is too short for Bremerton, take Bainbridge because it has more return trips than Vashon. Unfortunately, a dilemma awaits you at the Ferry's end: there ain't a darn thing to do in Bainbridge or Vashon once you reach the other side. But don't feel guilty about it, as Vent says, "it's the Ferry that matters" – just exit the ferry and turn back around. Or, perhaps if you drive inland you will find a restaurant or ice cream parlor. Worse, you can subject yourself to the Bloedel Reserve on Bainbridge. This beautifully serene arbore*tum* even has a bird refuge your mother-in-law would love; but it fails terribly on the Bore-o-Meter, so leave this one to the grandparents. The only option remaining is to drive aimlessly and regard the pastoral landscape. You may wonder why you didn't buy a beach getaway in the 80s, (or Microsoft stock in the 90s), but you'll kill a few hours in the process.

PIER 52 FERRY TERMINAL

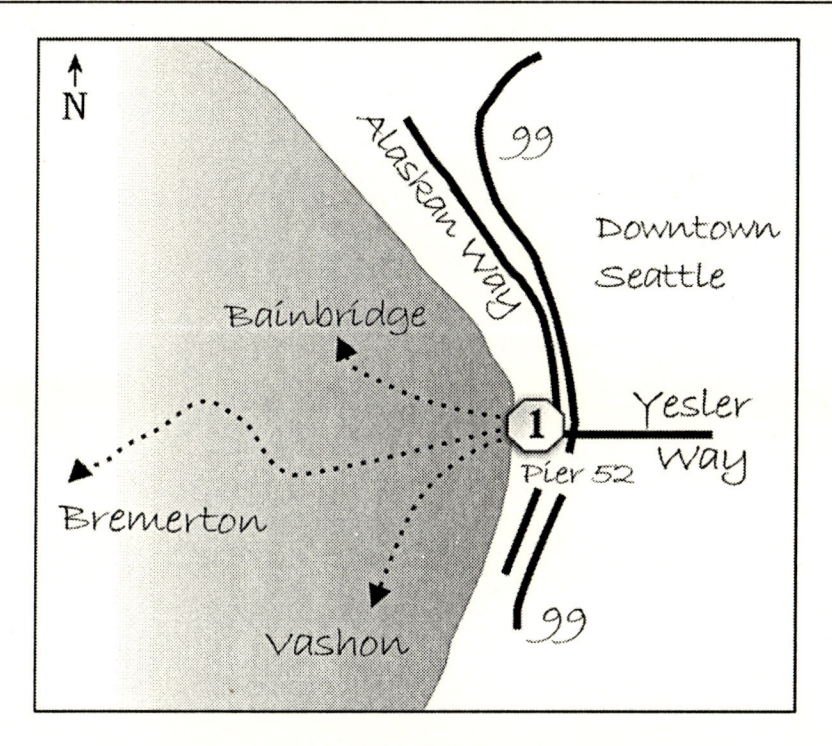

1. Ferry Terminal - Pier 52 off Alaskan Way
   http://www.wsdot.wa.gov/ferries (206) 464-6400

Ean Vent

"It is not only for what we do that we are held responsible,
but also for what we do not do."
–Moliere

6. Pipes, Pipes...Greenwood Car Show

Once a year on a summer Saturday, the Greenwood'ers come out of the woodwork with their hotrods and pristine classics. Fifteen blocks of people, pipes, and chrome fill the main drag. Kids love cars, and guys love cars, so this is a no-brainer outing. Just park, and walk around – the Bore-o-Meter takes care of the rest.

Movement	■■■■■
Machinery	■■■■■
Loudness	■■■■■
Largeness	■■■■☐
Food	■■☐☐☐
Sugar	■■■☐☐
Rhythm	■■■■☐

Bore-o-Meter: 4.0

Machinery, Largeness, and Loudness hit red line; especially when the testosterone boils and a hot-rod owner can't help cranking up his supercharged 454. Food leaves a bit to be desired, however Sugar is plentiful. Be sure to stop at one of the Fireman stands and enjoy some cookies and lemonade and shoot the hoot with the big men.

You can keep up the Rhythm by walking a few blocks, eating a treat, and then rest in the shade. Better yet, steal someone's chair when they temporarily leave their post. Kids love pretending it's their car; but beware, the stodgy Classic car owners (rightfully) won't want your kids touching their cars – so don't let it happen! Best case, you probably already know someone (who knows someone, who knows someone) with a car at the show. The kids will be psyched when they find it, and perhaps sit in it, or near it. Later you'll overhear them bragging, "my dad's friend's hotrod at the show…"

✶Although the Fireman's cookies and lemonade do hit the spot, the best kid-friendly and dad-friendly establishment in Greenwood is Wing Dome. You still might need a fireman around after eating the spicy 7-alarm wings, but water comes for free (and pitchers of beer can be requisitioned). Although packed on car show day, this is a great way to spice up your outing. You won't find a kids menu at this mostly male grease-fest, but the "Dome" works anytime because rowdy kids go unnoticed. Plus, several televisions cover the days sporting events.

✶At the end of the show (around 4:00 PM), you can bump your Loudness factor by 10x when the owners rev up their engines. Enjoy the roar and then watch the machinery on the move. Quickly get to your car, and join in on the action. Play a little car tag by zipping around Greenwoods' alleys and backstreets – kids love the chase. Anything with flames, catch it. Anything looks fast, pass it. Any old classic, follow it. You won't find a Seattle afternoon with cooler cars out on the road. Happy hunting.

GETTING TO GREENWOOD

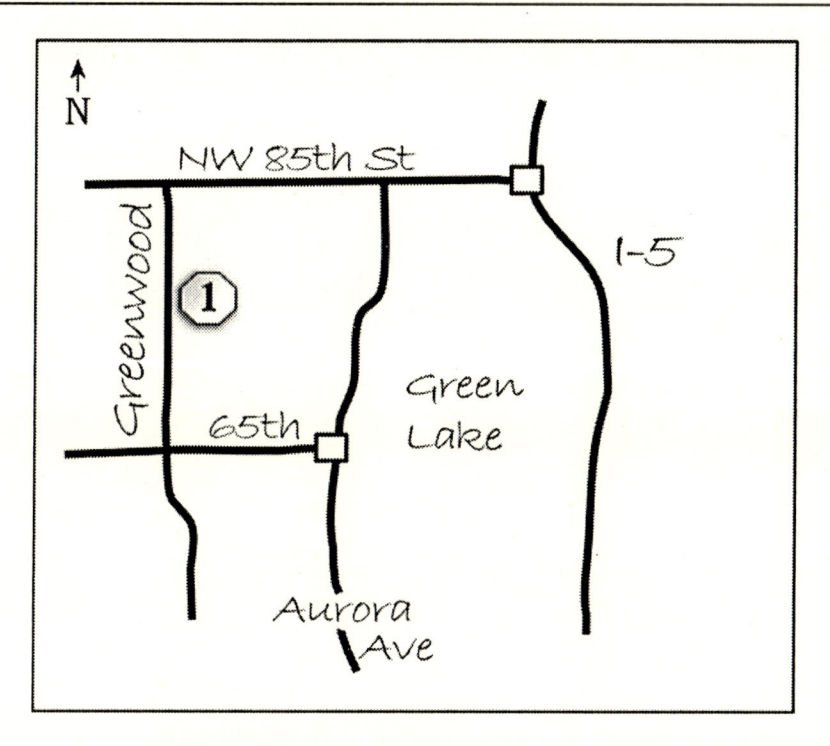

1. **Greenwood Car Show** – on Greenwood Ave N between NW 85th St and NW 65th St.
   http://www.greenwood-phinney.com (206) 789-1148

Ean Vent

7. The Need For Speed - Evergreen Speedway

This outing will knock your socks off. Squealing tires, thundering noise, and that home town feeling that can only emanate from old fashioned ball parks (or race tracks in this case). The wooden bleachers, cheap popcorn, and cheesy announcers add a fun local flair. Just replace the crisp green grass of a baseball diamond with black asphalt and extreme figure eight racing and you've got yourself a perfect 5.0 on the Bore-o-Meter.

Movement	■■■■
Machinery	■■■■
Loudness	■■■■
Largeness	■■■■
Food	■■■■
Sugar	■■■■
Rhythm	■■■■

Bore-o-Meter: 5.0

On Saturday nights, head north to the Evergreen Speedway in Monroe (off of Highway 2 just west of the 522 interchange) and catch the action: Bombers, Stingers, Hornets, figure 8s, and Nascar Super Stocks (that look close to the real thing). Just sit back and let the noise do the work.

These local heroes really juice it down the straights and smoke around the corners. Somehow the figure 8 drivers barely avoid T-bones at full speed, while the crowd holds its breath. Then the funky yellow Hornets buzz around the track and rev up the 4 cylinders on the stretch. And the Nascar B's display some impressive racing moves on the big track. Any style of racing is guaranteed to please, and the kids can't get enough. It could be a late night, but they'll beg for weeks to return with their friends, cousins, and mommy.

*If you head to the track an hour before the main event (typically around 6pm), the drivers park their cars down on the track for autographs and pictures. This provides a real treat for the kids and a moment of fame for the local drivers. You'll acquire a few blurry dot-matrix print outs signed by the drivers, and maybe a free t-shirt. Perhaps a driver will slap a racing helmet on your kid and hoist them into the driver's seat – now this gets the racing mood started right.

"hmmm, the art history museum, or extreme figure 8's...You decide."

Keep an eye on http://www.evergreenspeedway.com for special events guaranteed to blow your mind. The end of season extravaganza can't be missed. On this special night, insanity reigns with school bus figure-eights, roll over contests (no joke), 3-car train races, demo derby, and boat smashups. Rain or shine, the testosterone in the crowd will be raging.

The roll over contest features tiny beaters such as a Subaru Justy or a clunky Hundai that hit a four foot ramp with one wheel at top speed. Top speed for these crafts ranges from 5 miles an hour with the help of a push-truck, to a good 35-40 mph crash. Drivers must turn the car sideways to achieve as many rolls as possible. Three to four is good, five or six gets into record territory. Ambulances are standing by, but crazily the cars often land on their feet and can drive away – kids, don't try this at home!

The real insanity starts when the school buses hit the scene. Some sport massive bumpers, others funky horns, and some don't even have doors. They race around the figure 8 track at good speed with definite crash action: bumper-bashes, spin-outs, blow-outs, roll-overs, and high speed T-bones – it's all legal here.

If that doesn't tempt your palate, the three-car-trains come out with a driver in the front, a driver in the rear, and luckily, no driver in the middle car. The goal here is to win the race, but often the drivers will forgo half the track and repeatedly attempt a T-bone bash with the current leader. It's a cat and mouse game but inevitably the rear driver gets mauled. Then the boats come out, strapped to the back of the cars and all the gloves come off. I'd love to tell all, but that would spoil the fun. Just go experience it.

✻You can also plan your trip to the racetrack to coincide with the Evergreen State Fair. Near the end of August and Labor Day weekend you'll find events going on all day long: pig races, hula hoop contests, horse shows, roping contests, a petting farm, magicians, and the can't miss "Swine Costume" class.
http://www.evergreenfair.org (360) 805-6700

✻The "Reptile Man" Scott Petersen also runs a Serpentar*ium* in Monroe just a bit farther west on Highway 2. Home to a wild array of reptilian creatures: alligators, snakes, crocodiles, lizards, and even a two headed turtle. http://www.reptileman.com (360) 668-8204

EVERGREEN SPEEDWAY

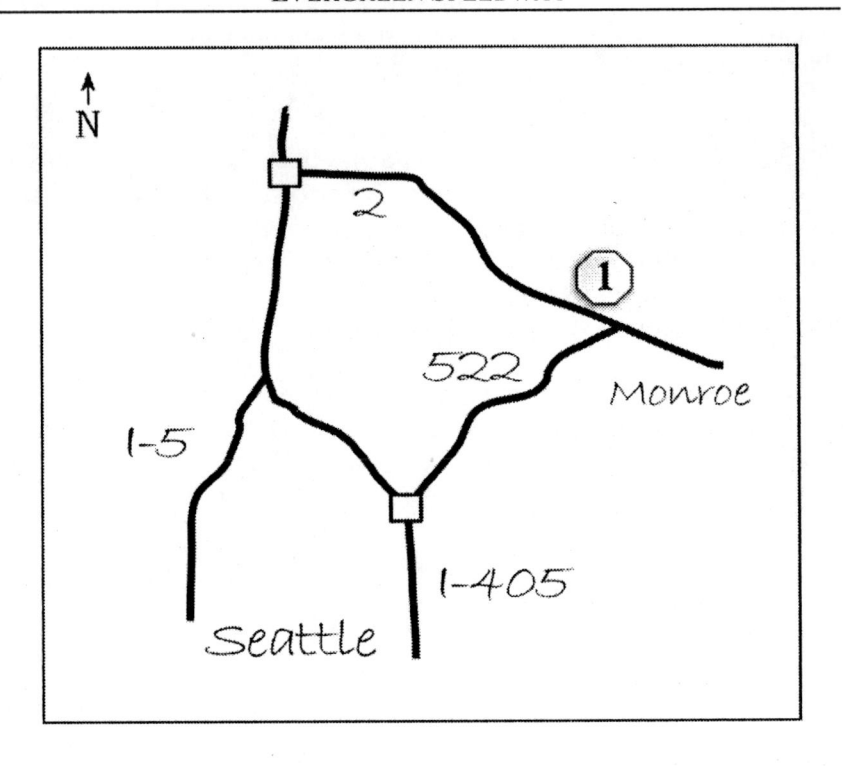

1. **Evergreen Speedway** – North of Seattle outside Monroe, off HW 2, just west of the highway 522 interchange. www.evergreenspeedway.com (360) 805-6100

8. Seafair – Blue Angels & Hydros

Prepare yourself for a new level of loudness. The Blue Angels provide the class of sound you don't actually hear, but only feel. Each time a snazzy blue and yellow F/A-18 Hornet zips above your head (with 16000 pounds of thrust pumping from each turbofan engine), a wall of soul shaking sound follows. And when all six jets buzz the boats in tight delta formation over Lake Washington... Ahh, it's a beautiful thing. Then to top it off, the hydroplanes rip it up around the lake for more delightful entertainment. The kids will remain stunned for weeks.

Movement	■■■■■
Machinery	■■■■■
Loudness	■■■■■
Largeness	■■■■■
Food	■■■■■
Sugar	■■■■■
Rhythm	■■■■■

Bore-o-Meter: 5.0

Coming to you faithfully each year in August for Sea Fair, this is a must-do Dad Duty event. The big air show happens on Saturday and Sunday around noon, and the hydros will be racing all day. The best spot to watch the festivities is from the water on your 30 foot Bayliner – or your buddies. But if you don't have access to a boat, carve out a grassy spot somewhere on Lake Washington near I-90 (with the rest of the 300,000+ crowd) and take it all in. The hydros race just south of I-90 at Stan Sayres Memorial Park, and traffic gets nightmarish the closer you go towards the park, but what's your rush? Bring a picnic lunch, blankets, hats, and of course, the sun screen because staring up at the sky all day takes its toll.

VENTS

"Avoiding the parking fiasco does not work as justification to buy a yacht, trust me."

While the weekend remains the most popular, Friday offers a sneak-peak if you can ditch work for a while. Grab the kids and dive into the world of the hydros. Take the pit tour and check out the hydro teams tuning their engines, doing preliminary races, and talking shop. Also, the Blue Angels close down I-90 all week around lunch for practice, so you can catch some G's too if your timing lines up. If ditching work is a no-can-do, you can likely get into the pits on the weekend too, but be prepared for a crowd.

Dad Duty Seattle

It's no surprise this outing bursts the Bore-o-Meter in Movement, Machinery, Loudness, and Largeness. A no contest 5.0 so long as you grab some treats and sweets on the way. Do you need more convincing? Do your kids a favor and subject them to fighter jets and hydro racing all in one day, they'll appreciate it.

✳ Catch the Navy Fleet when they roll into town to kick off the big Seafair weekend. Watch the Seafair website (http://www.seafair.com) for tour scheduling. You can explore these awesome vessels with your kids and really pump the Largeness and Machinery categories. Any of the ships offer interesting facts and fun, but if a carrier comes to town don't miss it. The hugeness of these boats can't be overstated. Plus, the Blue Angels just might perform a fly-by while practicing for their show. A tip of six wings in unison while you're standing on the deck of a Navy ship packed with air craft and helicopters... Priceless.

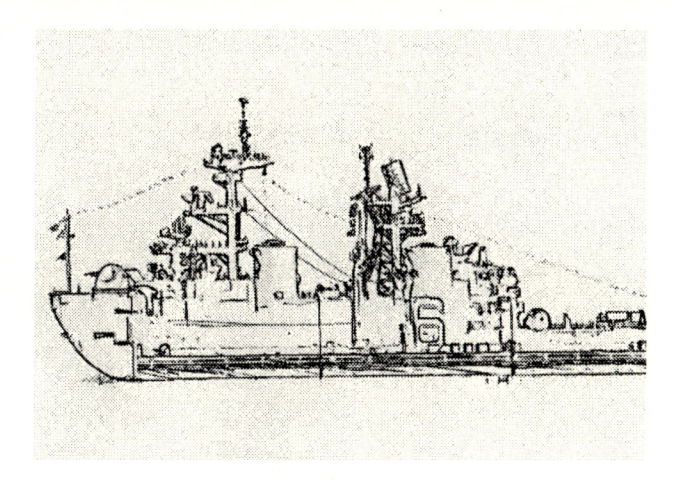

WATCHING THE BLUE ANGELS & HYDROS

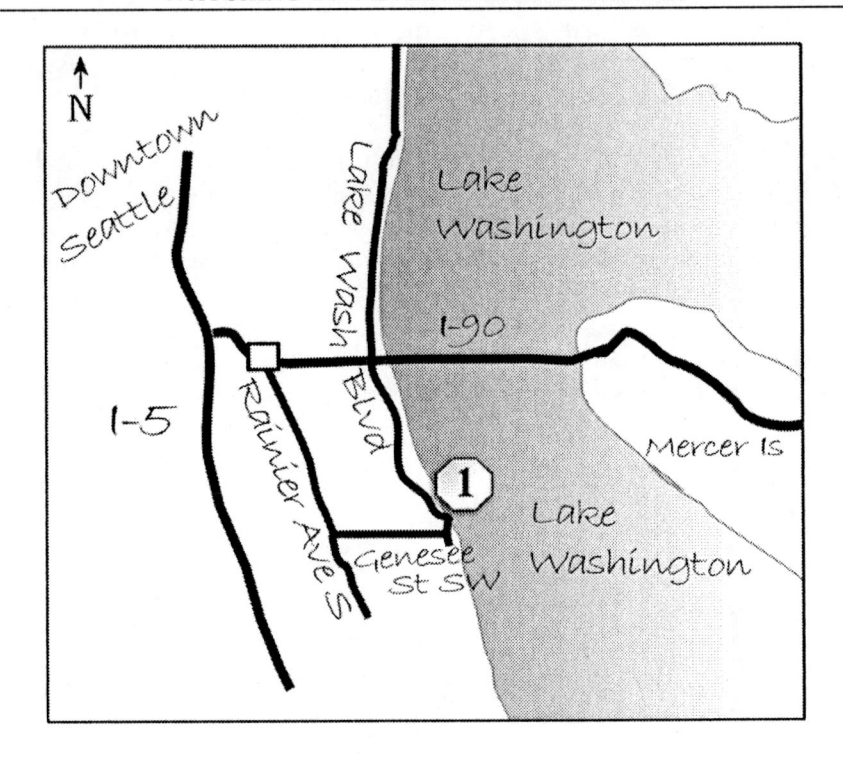

1. **Stan Sayres Memorial Park** –Hydros are off Lake Washington Blvd between 43rd and 46th Ave S. http://www.seafair.com (206) 728-0123

Dad Duty Seattle

"VENTS / VENTS" "Been there, done that? Then why are you reading this guide book..."

~

"We never know the joy of the parent,
till we become parents ourselves."
–Henry Ward Beecher

9. SNOQUALMIE CALLS

When cabin fever strikes and it's time to get the heck out of Dodge, head for Snoqualmie Falls. No preparation required, just strap in the kids and start driving east on I-90. This outing won't blow your mind but beats McDonald's play-land any day. Prepare yourself for a waterfall 100 feet higher than Niagara, and an old school train ride on a big locomotive.

> Movement ■■■■
> Machinery ■■■■
> Loudness ■■■□
> Largeness ■■■■
> Food ■■□□
> Sugar ■■■□
> Rhythm ■■■□□

Bore-o-Meter: 4.0

The Northwest Railway Museum runs a train that heads up the track for a view at the falls, and then back down into North Bend. If fortune holds, you'll ride the old orange locomotive #201 and imprint a lasting memory of "big orange train" in your kid's psyche. Seventy-five minutes of clickety-clack heals any case of cabin fever.

Other than the train ride, the Railroad museum won't offer many thrills; they've done a great job but it is a Mu-*seum* after all and Vent *don't* like that much. But that's ok – the magnitude of the machinery scattered around outside tips the scales. Metal clunkers of all shapes and sizes form a railroad graveyard along the roadside. Why do kids delight in a rusty old steam engine and a dry-rotting caboose? Who knows – maybe it's just the thrill of imagining its hay-day when steam choked from the stack and the whistle blared.

The falls are located northwest of town on Railroad Ave. Once you reach the Falls you've got two choices: 1) take a brief look from the top and head back to the town candy shop, or 2) walk all the way to the bottom and make a hike out of it. Your choice depends on your energy level and mood of the kids. The hike could be a glorious jaunt through the forest, or an epic journey you won't ever repeat. Unfortunately 'down' comes first, and as the kids skip ahead with joy, you realize each step must later be reversed. The bottom provides closer views and water-spray if you pick your way close; but no matter what, the mile of 'up' beckons.

The Bore-o-Meter holds no qualms with Snoqualmie. Movement, Machinery, Loudness, and Largeness fulfill themselves nicely, and the Snoqualmie Falls Candy Factory (just across from the Railroad Museum) boasts the best caramel corn ever. Grab lunch and watch the candy makers do their thing. All in all, a 4.0 outing that works on any weekend day (because the trains only run on Saturday and Sunday).

✻Downtown Snoqualmie holds the Railroad Days every year along Railroad Ave. Join the fair atmosphere with face painting, puppets, magicians, classic cars, kickin' motorcycles, and good eats. Watch the full parade and don't miss the unique "Antenna Ball Drop" where a helicopter drops tons of balls filled with ice cream and prizes for the kids (and even train tickets if you're lucky). Although the dates may conflict with Sea Fair and the Blue Angels (ouch), try to catch the Railroad Days at least once. http://www.railroaddays.com

Dad Duty Seattle

GETTING TO THE FALLS

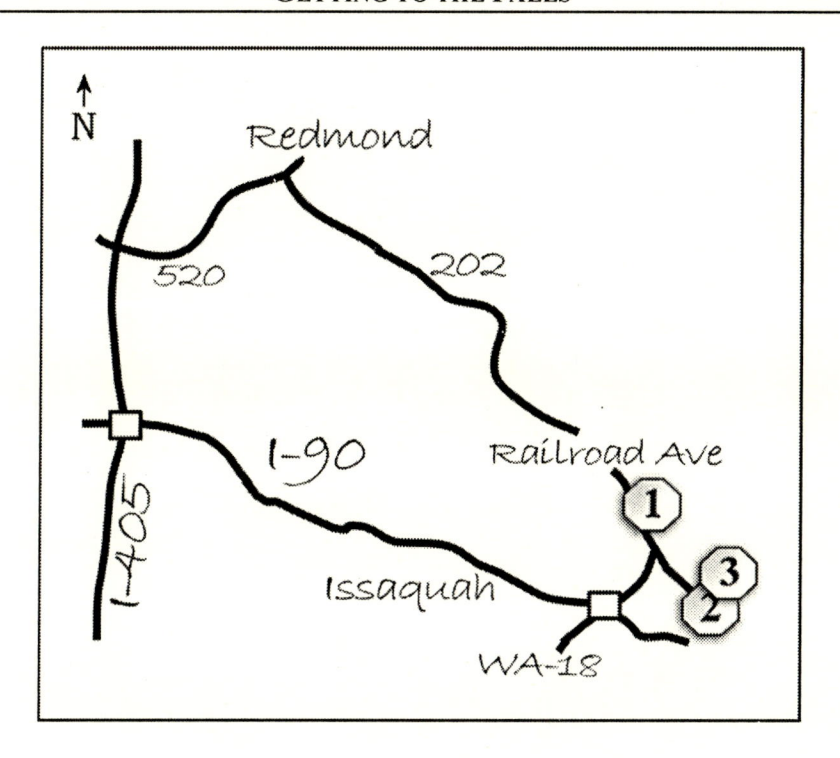

1. **Snoqualmie Falls** – 6501 Railway Ave SE
   http://www.snoqualmiefalls.com
2. **Snoqualmie Depot** – 38625 SE King Street
   http://www.trainmuseum.org (425) 888-3003
3. **Snoqualmie Candy Factory.** – 8102 Railway Ave SE
   http://www.snofallscandy.com (425) 888-0439

~

"The most important thing
that a man can do for his children,
is to love their mother"

–Theodore M. Hesburgh

10. ALKI BEACH DAY

Alki offers the Northwest version of a California beach scene: cyclists, skaters, scooters, and strollers pack the boardwalk, unmuffled Civics cruise the strip, leather clad males show off their motorcycles, and scantily dressed beach volleyball'ers bronze in the sun. All that's missing are the bikinis, the surfers, and the waves! But, throw in Seattle's city skyline on your right hand, and Puget Sound's ferry boats gliding past the Olympics on your left, and you've got something special.

Movement	■■■■
Machinery	■■□□
Loudness	■■■□
Largeness	■■■□
Food	■■■■
Sugar	■■■■
Rhythm	■■■■□

Bore-o-Meter: 3.85

Show up in West Seattle with a few spoons and a Styrofoam cup, and your day is done. Kids love hanging out on the Alki beach, digging in the sand and throwing rocks into the Sound. Or, if you're outing is less spur-of-the-moment, throw in the bikes and the Big Wheels and join the fray on the path. It doesn't get much better than a sandy afternoon followed by greasy burgers and fries, topped off with a sunset over the Olympics.

EVENTS

"Don't forget the sun screen, or you'll bring home lobsters."

The drive to West Seattle alone will take a load off your mind. If you happen to come from the North, take highway 99 instead of I-5 and catch the city and waterfront views over the viaduct. You'll pass the waterfront piers, the Smith Tower, the stadiums (the only allowed *iums* in Vent's book), and then the ship docks. Large red cranes work the even larger container ships, and stacks of containers line the roads like toy blocks. Once you traverse the West Seattle Bridge, take the Harbor Avenue exit and you've made it.

Along Harbor Ave, start watching for the Jack Block Park on your right after about a half mile. Watch for the red arched entrance that resembles a ship's keel (or a giant ribcage). If you reach Salty's you missed it. The park boasts nice bathrooms and a small sand pit with unique metal climbing buoys, but mostly your focus is the cement trail headed towards the water and a killer view.

Take the trail up and around the outer edge of the Port of Seattle, where it elevates over the polluted (but under restoration) fenced in beach area. Scooters work well on this trail, but it is also an easy walk. Soon you'll end at the red crane monument that overlooks the water and downtown Seattle. While enjoying the views, read the placards to learn how the Port of Seattle shaped the container shipping industry and became a port to reckon with.

When you've had enough of Jack Block, head back to the car and continue driving northwest. At any time you can park and enjoy the bike path that traverses the entire point; otherwise just regard the skyscrapers, container ships, and ferries across the water. When the condos stop, and the volleyball courts start, just park and find a free square of sand. Not much else to it – Enjoy!

✳Lots of room for Movement on this outing, and the Food and Sugar categories measure in at a solid 5.0. Top kid favorite goes to Pepperdocks for excellent greasy burgers and generous ice cream cones. No matter what, the Alki restaurant scene won't disappoint. Pizza, burgers, fish-n-chips, pastries, lattes, and brew pubs blanket the strip. How about Mexican, Thai, Italian, or seafood? The guide books can't keep up as the restaurant makeovers occur regularly; but whatever you want, Alki has got you covered.

Dad Duty Seattle

✷If the beach loses its fun; hit the Alki Playground a few blocks off the strip (on SW Lander St between 58th and 59th Street). Recently, the city overhauled all the play equipment with shiny new versions, and replaced the old wooden boat with a bland rubbery version. The new boat may boast safety and functionality, but definitely lost some character in the makeover.

✷ For a fabulous adventure in the old growth, visit the Schmitz Preserve Park. This slice of prime West Seattle real estate (and prime logging too) has managed to remain untouched since 1908. Thanks to "the Friends of Schmitz Park", you'll find excellent groomed trails with lots of short cuts and long cuts through the evergreens. The park is nestled off of Admiral Way as it heads back up to the top of West Seattle. Drive on any numbered street away from the strip (59th to 63rd) and you'll run into Admiral Way SW. Turn left up the hill and then watch for SW Stevens St. on your right. Park along the road and wander up the trails that switch back and forth across the ravine. As long as you remember that your vehicle is somewhere down and to the right, eventually you'll find it. For more information check out the http://www.shmitzpark.org or the Seattle's great parks website: http://www.cityofseattle.net/parks

ALKI

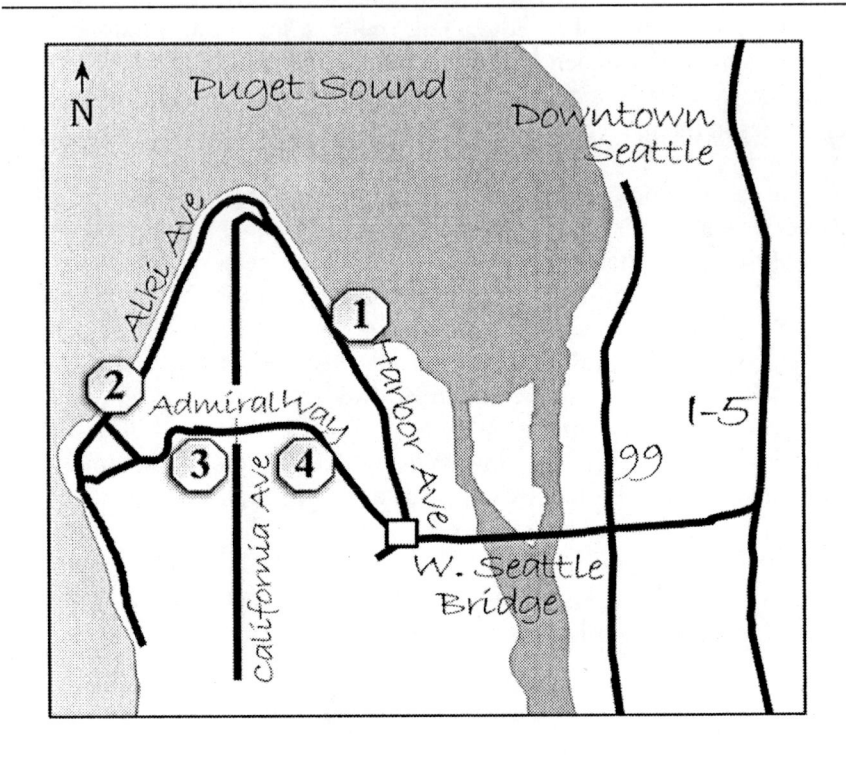

1. **Jack Block Park** – off Harbor Ave (east side of road).
2. **Alki Strip** – beach, restaurants, bike path
3. **Schmitz Preserve Park** - SW Stevens St & Admiral Way
4. **Belvedere Viewpoint** – fabulous city view off Admiral.

11. REMLINGER FARMS

All kids love pony rides and petting zoos, right? Remlinger Farms outside Carnation has got the goods. While the Bore-o-Meter won't jump off the charts when you're feeding the goats, you will score major Movement points at the kiddy amusement park. Take the steam train, ride the mini-coaster, and spin on the flying' pumpkins. There's also a covered hay maze, a mine to investigate, and live entertainment with singing and carrying on for the kids.

Movement	■■■■
Machinery	■■■□
Loudness	■■■□
Largeness	■■□□
Food	■■■□
Sugar	■■■□
Rhythm	■■■□

Bore-o-Meter: 4.0

Not much preparation for this outing, just drive east out 520 and highway 202 and take in the country extravaganza. Your kids might not brag to their friends for weeks to come, but it scores a solid 4.0 and there is nothing wrong with good clean family fun. A high success rate and the ability to knock off several hours with little effort put this outing on the Dad Duty docket.

VENTS / SUNAV
"What will they think of next? this tourist trap has it all."

Home style country cooking at the restaurant knocks off the Food category. And since the Sugar category can't be neglected, be sure to head to the Bakery for brownies or fresh cookies. Also, as this remains a working farm you can pick up farm fresh produce and a few cases of seasonal fruit. Don't forget a famous take-n-bake Remlinger Farms Pie. These babies are so good that you'll be tempted to take all the credit when the dinner guests rave about it. Just be sure to push the box way down under the recycling in case a conscientious guest cleans up and calls your bluff.

✷The October Fall Harvest festival does ya right. Make a day out of getting your pumpkins for Halloween. Ride the free wagon with hay bails, eat some pumpkin pie, and buy some Christmas crafts for the in-laws. Remlinger really goes the extra mile come harvest time.

✷Check out the online schedule at http://www.remlingerfarms.com for special events and to see what crop is in season. Better yet, sign up for the "Ripe-n-Ready" email list to get the all-points-broadcast for can't miss events like the opening day of strawberry season, or a new crop of Eastern Washington cantaloupe.

THE ROAD TO REMLINGER

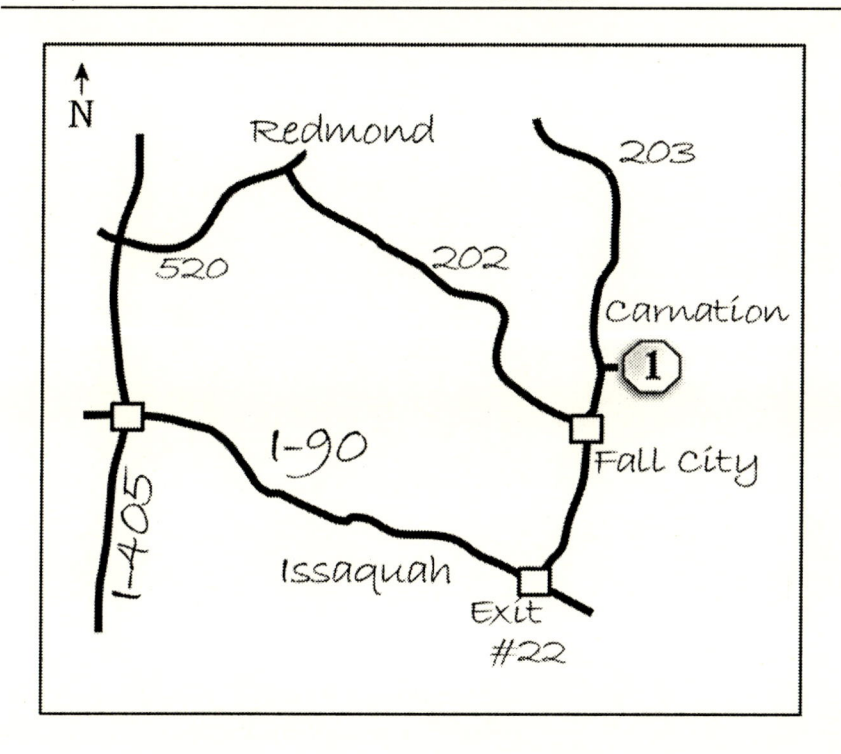

1. Remlinger Farms – off HW 203 on NE 32nd St. Watch for a sign at the turnoff, then dead end at the Farm. http://www.remlingerfarms.com (425) 333-4135

Ean Vent

Stadium - the only "ium" approved by Vent.

12. TAKE ME OUT TO THE... BALLGAME

Mariner's baseball wins hands down for best professional sport outing for kids. While any sporting event can pass the mustard, the atmosphere at the ballpark really works. Maybe the slow baseball pace lulls the crowd into civility – whereas with football or hockey you're sure to face a drunkard yelling obscenities in your kids' ear.

Movement	■■■■
Machinery	■■□□
Loudness	■■■■
Largeness	■■■■
Food	■■■■
Sugar	■■■■
Rhythm	■■■□

Bore-o-Meter: 4.42

Buy me some peanuts and cracker jacks, root-root-root for the home team, and you're living the song. But don't forget the garlic fries. The aroma can't be avoided, so you better join 'em because you can't beat 'em. Although when you arrive home in a garlic cloud, don't expect any good night smooches.

Your other ballpark task is to meet *the man*. Find a Dixie's BBQ stand for fantastic Que (not too hard since there are three of them). Then, add a few toothpicks of the nuclear hot sauce called "the man" onto your grub. As the story goes, this insane hot sauce originates from the auto-shop turned iconic barbeque shop in Bellevue. But beware: the slightest touch to the lip can make grown men cry.

Don't forget Rhythm at the ballpark. Your kid likely won't sit through the entire game, so take a break and walk around the stadium. Head to the Bull Pen in left field to watch the relievers warm up, hit the

Ean Vent

baseball themed kid's playground area in center field, and enjoy the city and water views from the upper deck. Buy some ice cream, an Ichiro jersey, and then head for home – there's no sin in leaving the game early on a high note.

✳Go early for batting practice and you can witness some serious slugging. The park opens exactly two hours prior to game time and there will be a line. Go directly to right field and get ready for some homeruns. Don't forget the baseball gloves, and the earlier you arrive, the better your chance to catch the long ball.

✳Tip: take only one child to the ballpark at a time if possible. The more squirmers, the more difficulties if you are on your own. Besides, one-on-one time with Daddy makes for solid memories. If this presents a problem, attempt to fortify your flank with more Dads, negotiate a rotation scheme, or throw in the towel and buy the family fun pack for Mom too.

SAFECO FIELD

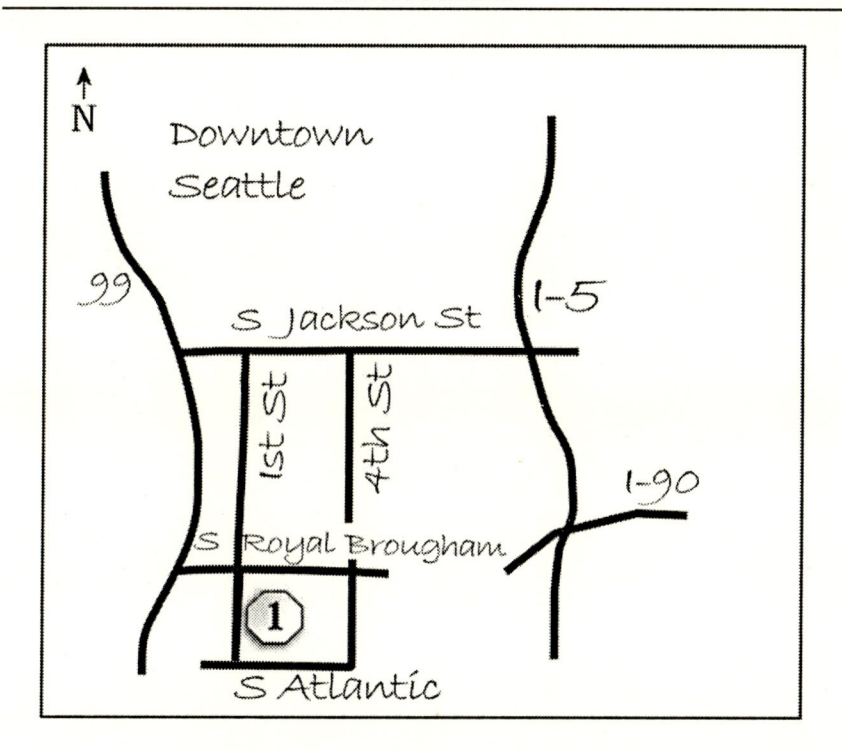

1. **Safeco Field** – 1250 First Avenue, Seattle
   http://seattle.mariners.mlb.com (206) 346-4001

Ean Vent

~

"We cannot choose how we are
going to die. Or when. But we can
decide how we are going to live. Now."

–Joan Baez

13. Emerald Ups & Downs

No time like the present to introduce your kids to the wonderful world of horse gambling. Seriously, going to the "Downs" holds good kid value, as well as a chance to donate your money. Just head south of Seattle on highway 167 for the fun. This outing favors adults a bit over kids; but if you pick a sunny summer Sunday afternoon you'll do well.

Movement	■■■■☐
Machinery	■■☐☐☐
Loudness	■■■■☐
Largeness	■■■■☐
Food	■■■■■
Sugar	■■■■■
Rhythm	■■■☐☐

Bore-o-Meter: 3.85

Throughout the summer on Sundays, Emerald Downs markets to families with free pony rides, face painting, furry mascots, and lots of eats and treats. Along with the racing, these extra events make the outing tick. Kids get a kick out of the big stadium, the bustling excitement, and watching the horses hit the track.

Walk down close to the track and the kids can pet the trainer horses waiting to escort the racers. Strike up some small-talk with the trainers and then head over to the Paddock to watch the circling parade of horses. Then listen to the bugler blow out the "Call to the Post" and get your bets in pronto before post time. Whether you box in an exacta, trifecta, or superfecta, or you pick 'em straight up to win, place, and show, the betting will keep you busy. A few minutes later: "They're off!"

VENTS "The only downer at the track:
30 minutes between races."

As Vent points out above, a half-hour of idle time followed by a half-minute of excitement won't amaze the kids for long. This is why the Sunday family days remain important to augment the races. Also focus on the mile races because the horses start and finish directly in front of the stands. The shorter six-furrow races start on the far side of the track and all the horses remain tiny dots until the last few lengths.

∗On an up note: garlic fries are back. All your standard stadium food makes the Bore-o-Meter smile. Largeness and Loudness do fairly well, and perhaps you could describe a horse as machinery, but this is where the Downs falls down a bit.

HEAD TO EMERALD DOWNS

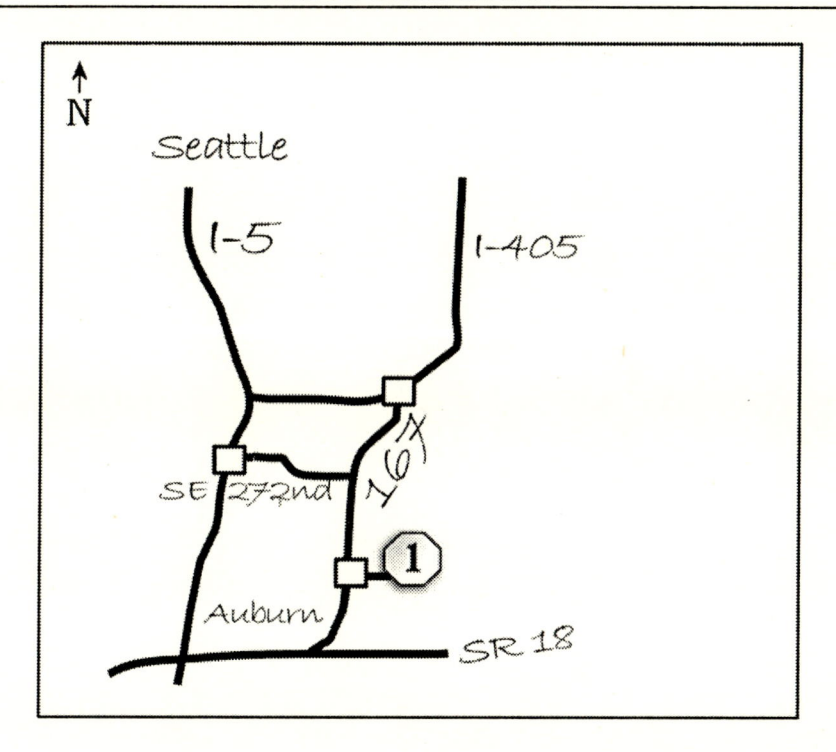

1. **Emerald Downs** – 2300 Emerald Downs Drive, Auburn off HW 167 turn onto 15th Street NW
http://www.emdowns.com (253) 288-7000

~

"Being a great father gives a woman entirely new ways to love her man."

–J Fleming

14. FUNTASIA DAZE YA

Picture Chuck E. Cheeses on steroids and you've got Funtasia. Albeit low on creativity, no where else can you enjoy a bumper boat water fight with random strangers. You may not score a ton of originality points, but these fun-fests make the Bore-o-Meter cut (and all you need is a credit card).

Movement	■■■■□
Machinery	■■■■□
Loudness	■■■■□
Largeness	■■■■□
Food	■■□□□
Sugar	■■■■□
Rhythm	■■■■□

Bore-o-Meter: 3.71

Take your pick: Funtasia to the north or Family Fun Center to the south. The Family Fun Center in South Center feels bigger and looks newer, but is often more crowded; whereas Funtasia on 99 in Edmonds sits more off the beaten track. Either spot satisfies the kids with golf, go-karts, games, and grub.

For the toddlers, pay a few bucks for the kiddie-land full of plastic toy fun. Otherwise, here's the drill: play some vids, empty your wallet, play some more vids, hit the ATM. Collect a ton of tickets and cash them in for worthless plastic wares.

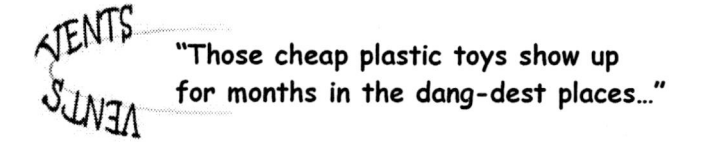

"Those cheap plastic toys show up for months in the dang-dest places..."

If your child passes the 33 inch cut, they can ride along on the Go-Karts. Show off your race car reflexes on cement tracks with banked turns and gas powered carts. Squeal some turns, and burn rubber baby. Then hit the bumper boats for a splash fest, and end off the day with putt-putt golf. You can easily knock off an hour or two for the unexpected *Dad Duty*. In the end you'll be dazed, but it beats the Children's museum any day.

*If your kids like amusement parks, check out the Bench Warmers section for other fun fests, fairs and amusement parks. Any of these establishments can entertain the tikes: Wild Waves Enchanted Park, Illusionz, Puyallup Fair down south, or Miniature World way up north.

FUNTASIA

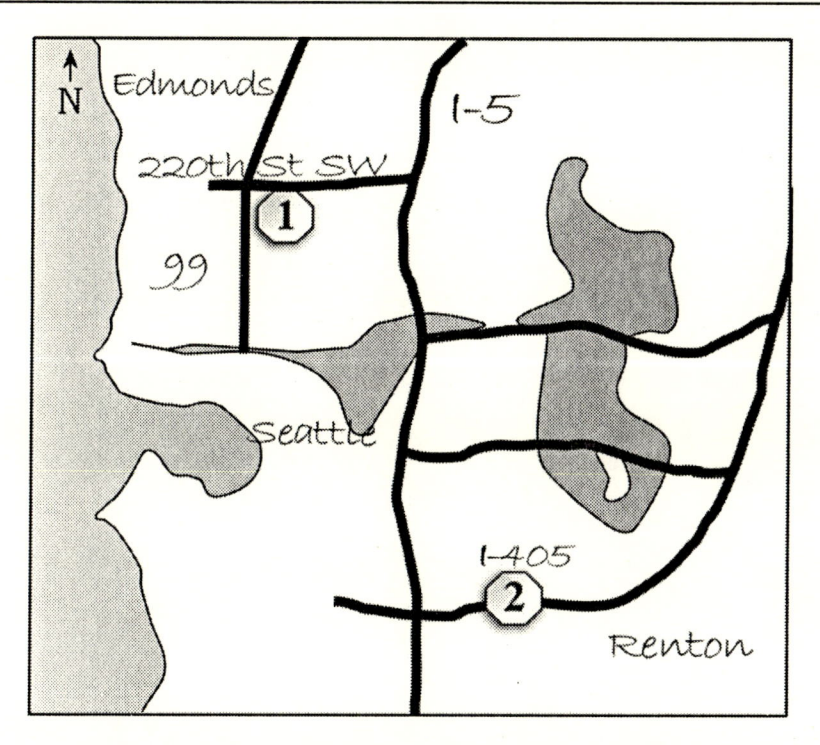

1. **Funtasia** – 7212 220th SW, Edmonds. On southeast corner of Hwy 99 and 220th St SW (exit #179 off I-5). http://www.familyfunpark.com (425)-775-2174

2. **Family Fun Center** – 7300 Fun Center Way, Tukwila. North of I-405 at Southcenter Blvd and W Valley HWY. http://www.fun-center.com (425) 228-7300

~

"Each day of our lives we make deposits
in the memory banks of our children"

–Charles Swindoll

15. MAKING TRACKS AT TRAXX

Traxx Racing remains the only Seattle area fun-fest where kids can hit the race track entirely on their OWN. That's right, Traxx Racing in Mukilteo features a kids track for ages three and up. While it remains a treat to drive your kid around shotgun at Funtasia, the Bore-o-Meter really pops when you plop a racing helmet and full suit on your child and send them out solo on the track. Plus, the wings, pizza, beer, jalapeno poppers and other happy-hour junk food far exceed the Funtasia fair.

Movement	■■■■■
Machinery	■■■■■
Loudness	■■■■■
Largeness	■■■■☐
Food	■■■■☐
Sugar	■■■■☐
Rhythm	■■■■■

Bore-o-Meter: 4.57

For kids, Traxx offers small electric karts for the three to five year olds, and cool little gas-powered karts for six through ten year olds. They provide genuine race helmets and a coverall racing suit to pump up the ambiance. Kids love the fierce competition, the thrill of victory (and the agony of defeat), and you'll hear lots of bragging about driving solo.

"Badges? We don't need no stinking badges..."

Once the racers hit eleven they can head out on the adult track after passing a permit class, and fourteen year olds are home free. The indoor quarter-mile adult track also boasts hairpin turns and a thrilling ramp that's at least 10 feet high. All laps are timed electronically and your ranking shows up on video monitors. Plus, there are indoor and outdoor tracks so rain or shine this remains a hit.

Traxx especially targets birthday parties with fun themed party packs and banquet rooms. Definitely Vent's pick for a birthday party; it far outdoes Build-A-Bear even on a bad day. Food and Sugar are covered in one sweep with the race car shaped hotdogs with chocolate donut wheels and checkered flags. Or score a burger and fries in a flaming hotrod container. In addition, there's a climbing wall, a bouncy basketball contraption, and obligatory video games to keep you busy.

As if the Go-Karts weren't enough, this is likely the only race track on the planet featuring motorized toilet racing. You can take on the obstacle course and race your friends while sitting on the pot. Visit Traxx online for all the details at http://www.traxxracing.org.

✷ Check out other racing fun in the Bench Warmers section. The only other known establishment where kids can ride solo is Miniature World near Birch Bay and Bellingham. They feature "Kidz-Karts" and any trip up north deserves your attention. Then, when the kids hit their teens you can try out Champs for serious racing fun.

TRAXX RACING IN MUKILTEO

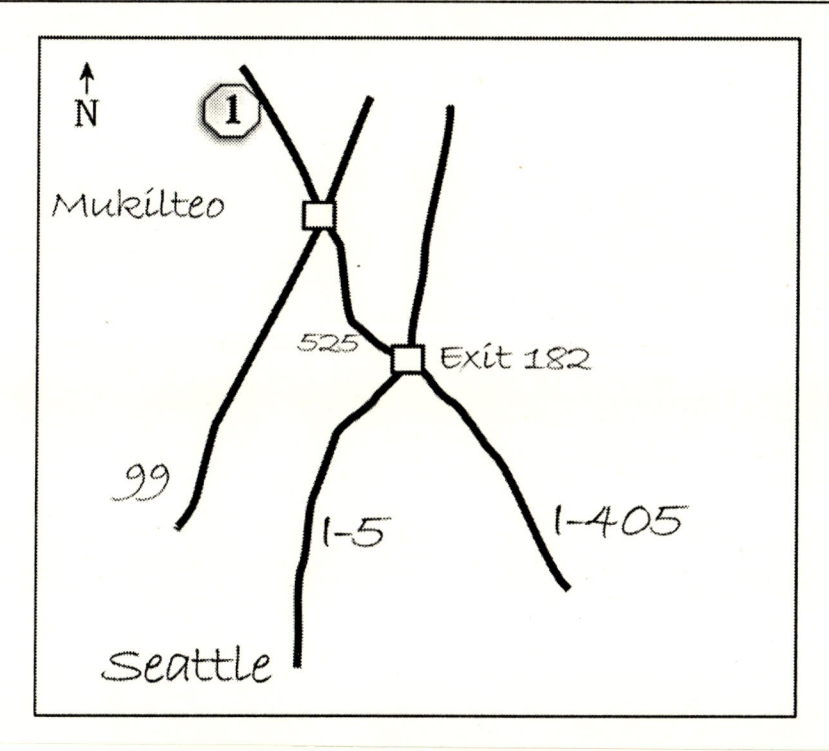

1. **Traxx Racing** – North of Seattle in Mukilteo. Take exit 182 off I-5, stay on highway 525 (Mukilteo Speedway) to 4329 Chennault Beach Road. www.traxxracing.com (425) 493-8729

VENTS
VENTS

"Motorized Toilet Racing: the next Olympic sport."

16. Pacific Raceways Extravaganza

Amongst the gentle rolling hills south of Seattle, you'll find a beautiful Northwest landscape – and, a full-fledged racetrack tucked between the giant evergreens! The Pacific Raceways track in eastern Kent delivers adrenalin packed racing for all fancies: motocross, drag racing, and road racing.

Movement	■■■■■
Machinery	■■■■■
Loudness	■■■■■
Largeness	■■■■■
Food	■■□□□
Sugar	■■□□□
Rhythm	■■■■□

Bore-o-Meter: 4.14

Friday night hosts the local motocross races where hoards of moto-folks dressed in their moto-gear descend on the dirt track. Full families get in on the action, and the young ones nail the jumps just like the big guys. Your kids may plug their ears at first but they'll soon be whooping it up.

This local affair remains highly regarded by the Bore-o-Meter. The riders juicing their bikes in the parking area alone take care of Machinery, Movement, and Loudness. Food does exist, but bring cash because the concession tent filled with folding chairs and fresh cooked dogs won't be accepting your credit card. Who knows, you may soon invest in a 50cc mini-bike for your four year old and set 'em loose on the short track.

When the motocross excitement wears off, see if the drag strip is running open races. Friday night your motocross ticket ought to get you in for free. Catch the local muscle cars hit 110mph, and the street bikes push 150mph. For real drags, check the Pacific Raceways online schedule for the NHRA races throughout the year.

Ean Vent

Better yet, try the "All Harley" Motorcycle drag races. These guys strap themselves to a nitrogen-burning rocket and blast down the track at 200 miles per hour! Picture a solo rider atop a metal cage with a single fat rear tire ripping up the asphalt. Loud and proud, these Harleys are music to the ears.

Pacific also boasts a full race track with full-on stock car races, vintage cars, and bikes. The knee-scraping motorcycle racers zip right by the fence at insane speeds.

*If all the racing is not enough, try to witness the 300 foot world record motorcycle jump. 2004 and 2005 featured Ryan Capes' massive jump – the Northwest's own Evil-Kneivel.

Watch http://www.pacificraceways.com for details.

Dad Duty Seattle

PACIFIC RACEWAYS

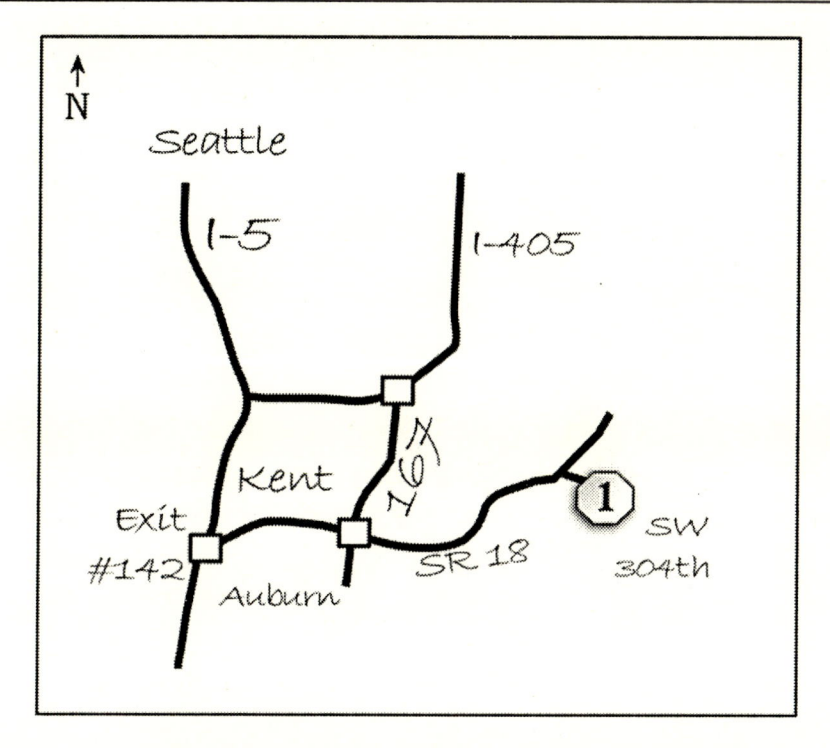

[Hand-drawn map showing Seattle with I-5 and I-405 converging near Kent, Exit #142 near Auburn, SR 18 heading east, and location 1 marked near SW 304th. Route 167 runs north-south.]

1. **Pacific Raceways** – 31001 144th Ave SE, Kent WA SE304th/SE 312th exit off SR18, then first left, first right. www.pacificraceways.com (253) 639-5927

"Don't forget about Rhythm.
It truly is the most important."

DAD DUTY CHEAT SHEET

Outing	Rating	When	Duration	Drive Time*
Downtown	4.7	Anytime (weekends)	2-5 hrs	5 min
Ballard	4.28	Anytime	2-3 hrs	15 min
Dump run	4.7	Anytime	2-3 hrs	11 min
Green Lake	3.85	Anytime	2 hrs	14 min
Ferry escape	4.0	Anytime	3-4 hrs	11 min
Greenwood Car show	4.0	Annual (July)	1-2 hrs	19 min
Evergreen Speedway	5.0	Saturday Nights	3-5 hrs	42 min (Monroe)
Blue Angels & Hydros	5.0	Annual (August)	3-5 hrs	17 min
Snoqualmie Falls	4.0	Weekends	2-3 hrs	30 min (East I-90)
Alki	3.85	Anytime	1-3 hrs	15 min
Remlinger Farms	4.0	Anytime (October)	2-4 hrs	30 min (Carnation)
Mariners	4.42	Baseball Season	1-3 hrs	10 min
Emerald Downs	3.85	Summer Sundays	2-3 hrs	32 min (Auburn)
Funtasia Daze Ya	3.71	Anytime	1-2 hrs	22 min (North 99)
Traxx Racing	4.57	Anytime	2-4 hrs	31 min (Mukilteo)
Pacific Raceways	4.14	Weekends, Friday Eve	3-5 hrs	43 min (S. Kent)

all drive times are calculated from I-5 & Mercer St. downtown (and it's not rush hour, a major sporting event, or a WTO riot)

"When shooting video, never exceed a 10 second clip. Preferably less."

BENCH WARMERS

In addition to the outings that made the Bore-o-Meter cut above, Seattle offers a rich selection of local attractions and events throughout the year (if you pay attention). These ideas can ride the pine until your starters need a rest. Here's Vents picks, in no particular order:

Woodland Park Zoo – "Must-do the Zoo." If animals registered on the Machinery scale this would've made the Bore-o-Meter cut no problem. Great rhythm, no preparation, and high on the repeatability scale. Purchase a yearly membership and enjoy. The main entrance is off 50th St. and Fremont Ave. (Watch http://www.thezoo.org for special events.)

✳After the zoo, grab some pizza at Vents favorite: **Crash Landing** on 7th and NW 65th St. Just head west down the hill for hot slices with no wait at this local favorite. Or, if you're up for a wait, go to **Zeeks** on 60th and Phinney Ridge: loud and kid-friendly with great salads and several TVs.

Seattle Parks - the Seattle city park system includes top-notch parks, trails, playgrounds, and beach access. Right in the middle of the city, you can find slices of preserved old growth trees and cool trails. Top picks: West Seattle's Schmitz Preserve, Discovery Park, Carkeek Park, North Beach Ravine, and Golden Gardens. These quick escapes immediately transform you from city life into the deep green rain forest, and kids dig it. The city website is a great resource: http://www.cityofseattle.net/parks

Community Centers - almost every neighborhood boasts a center with open gyms, toddler rooms, activities, and pools. It's a good bet yours is listed here: Alki, Ballard, Bitter Lake, Delridge, Garfield, Green Lake, Hiawatha, High Point, International District, Jefferson, Laurelhurst, Loyal Heights, Magnolia (*great pool), Magnuson, Meadowbrook, Miller, Montlake, Queen Anne, Rainier, Rainier Beach,

Ravenna-Eckstein, South Park, Southwest, Van Asselt, and Yesler. http://www.cityofseattle.net/parks/centers/

Freemont Solstice Parade - Don't miss the Solstice Parade in Fremont in mid June. The locals really impress with extravagant floats and costumes that took weeks and even months to prepare. (And, some costumes that only took a few seconds to take off!) Yes, the nude bikers will be on display – but most are doused in body paint anyway so it's all fun.

Kid friendly coffee – **Tully's** generally has toys, and **Harvest Bread Company** remains a winner. Plus, several local coffee joints thrive on their kid focus. Try the **Firehouse** in Ballard on 2622 N.W. Market St., and **Cloud City Coffee House** on 88th and Roosevelt Way NE.

Arrival of the Navy Fleet - catch the fleet arrival for SeaFair at the beginning of August. Definitely find your way onto one of the ships for a tour, and possibly even a ride around the sound. Watch the website http://www.seafair.com for the details and go salute the troops.

Green Lake Milk-Carton Derby – this event deserves your attendance at least once. It's a boat race with one stipulation: all crafts must be constructed from milk cartons! Creativity reigns, and you'll see it all: paddle boats made out of spare bike parts, wind-powered crafts, feet-powered crafts, kid-powered crafts, and lots of themed ships with an emphasis on cows, all floating on milk cartons of some sort. It's a wild event and sure to be a fun afternoon. Better yet, create your own entry!
http://www.seafair.com

Farmers Markets – just about every neighborhood offers a farmers market where the kids get good treats, and you can pick up some Washington veggies. http://www.seattlefarmersmarkets.org

Climbing Gyms – **REI** downtown has the huge climbing rock, a kid's play area on 2nd floor, and World Wraps at the top for good eats. **Stone Gardens** (on 2839 N.W. Market St) in Ballard and **Vertical World** (near Fisherman's Terminal on 2123 W. Elmore St,) both offer great kids climbing fun. Not cheap, but the kids love it, and you can go for monthly rates or join the structured training programs for kids 5 and up. If you plan to belay your child, Vent recommends a 1-1 ratio of parent-to-child; otherwise you won't be able to manage your other children while you are busy *on-belaying*. (This typically requires passing a certification test).
http://www.rei.com/stores/seattle
http://www.stonegardens.com
http://www.verticalworld.com

Golf Range – your kid may love hitting balls at the driving range. Try **Interbay** between Magnolia and Queen Anne, or any **Putz** driving ranges around town. Likely, you can find a loaner club and if the sport takes, invest in your own mini-iron.

Tacoma Dome – can't avoid the call of the mud. Keep an eye on the dome for Monster Trucks and Motocross events. You'll be glad you did.

The Puyallup Fair – a modest drive south (around 1 hour), but everybody must "Do the Puyallup" at least once. Tons of carnival rides, animals, exhibits, entertainment, and people. A real cash burner, but a good time (and you can try to knock over those darn milk jugs again at $2 a pop). Check out the schedule at http://www.thefair.com.

Wild Waves Enchanted Village – if you like theme parks, head to a bigger show at Enchanted Village. This one falls under the Six Flags hat and the admission fee hits the wallet a little harder. Located south of Seattle on I-5 and exit 142-B, it features roller coasters, bigger thrill rides, and a full size water park. Be prepared for a full day outing to make it worth it. (Vent recommends this for the older kids, although there are plenty of kiddie rides, it is tough to keep track of everyone at this circus). http://www.sixflags.com/parks/enchantedvillage

Illusionz in Issaquah – (more Fun Fests) In addition to the **Family Fun Center** in South Center, and **Funtasia** (gonna daze ya) in Edmonds off 99, try Illusionz on the east side (1025 NW Gilman Boulevard, Issaquah). It sports a unique magic theme and even a waterfall that falls *up*. Lasertag, putt-putt, climbing wall, kids magic castle, and a full set of arcades. http://www.illusionz.com

Miniature World – another go-kart establishment featuring "Kidz-Karts" is up at Miniature World near Birch Bay and Bellingham (exit 270 up I-5 North). A healthy drive north, but this remains the only other known fun center where kids can drive entirely on their own (besides Traxx Racing in Mukilteo). Also there is miniature golf, and a mini train ride that gets high kid marks. If you're heading up north, put this one on the list. http://www.miniatureworld.org

Champs Karts - once your youngsters hit age twelve, introduce them to Champs for serious kart racing. High powered electronic karts on challenging courses with a nifty electronic scoring system. Be sure to pick a cool race name as Champs saves your scores across multiple visits. You can even check your lifetime average online. Three locations: south downtown, Redmond, and Bothell. http://www.champskarting.com

Sporting Events – just about any sport event with a good fan base and noise will do. Try your local high school for wrestling, basketball, football, volleyball, track, and swim meets.

Bowling – most of the local bowling alleys have kid rails that make bowling a hit. This makes a good birthday party outing too. Leilani Lanes in Greenwood is Vents pick (10201 Greenwood Ave N). Smoke free on the weekends until the evening, and the kid rails are great. http://www.leilanilanes.com

Dad Duty Seattle

Ice Skating & Hockey– skating provides quick fun anytime. Plus, if a hockey game starts up after the public skate, stick around for it – the kids like the action (and the Zamboni). As you drive north, the skating rinks get newer and fancier. Starting on Aurora and 180th you'll find Highland Ice Arena (18005 Aurora Ave N). Much nicer is Lynnwood Ice Center (19803 68th Ave NW), and nicer yet: Everett Events Center (2000 Hewitt Ave in Everett). The public arena is called Comcast Community Skate Rink.
http://www.lynnwoodicecenter.com
http://www.highlandice.com
http://www.everetteventscenter.com

The Museum of Flight – if you must visit a museum, hit the museum of flight at Boeing Field south of downtown off I-5 (exit 186, on 128th to 100th) Check out the Concorde supersonic jet, Air Force one, and Blue Angels simulator. Enjoy the Largeness of this great attraction. If only they would've named it the "Tribute" to Flight, or the "Big Building" of Flight this could've made the Bore-o-Meter cut. Good repeatability too. http://www.museumofflight.org

Ride The Ducks – this half-bus half-boat tour of Seattle on a genuine World War II amphibious vehicle rates quite high with the toddlers. Especially great if you're not familiar with the downtown area, you'll pass by all the Bore-o-Meter hot spots starting from Seattle Center: Westlake, the Waterfront, Smith Tower, and Pioneer Square. Then you'll head north to Lake Union past Gas Works Park and dip into the water with fantastic cityscape views and float planes overhead. This is a great way to pick up some touristy Seattle trivia and knock off close to two hours no problem. The ticket booth is on the northeast corner of 5th and Broad across from the Space Needle. (206)-441-DUCK
http://www.ridetheducksofseattle.com

THAT'S A WRAP

Armed with the approved Dad Duty outings, and using the Bore-o-Meter as your own personal gauge, you're guaranteed some priceless memories. As a dad with young kids, this is your opportunity to shine, so take advantage of it. If you can pull off all the outings in this book with your children, consider yourself a star. Most likely, mom could use the break; or better yet, take your woman along for the ride. Enjoy!

✶ Be sure to check out *www.DadDuty.com* for the latest info, feedback, and discussion. Watch the calendar for coming attractions and reminders. Join the forums and talk shop. Read comments from the field by other dads, and leave your own battle stories. Got any outings that burst the Bore-o-Meter's bubble? Come online and post it.

"Life moves pretty fast. If you don't stop
and look around once in awhile,
you could miss it."

–Ferris Bueller

About the Author

Ean Vent has lived in Seattle for the last decade. He holds a B.S in Computer Science and Masters in Software Engineering, but that doesn't hold a candle to the challenges and joys of parenthood. When not stuck in a cubicle programming software, you can find him tooling around town with his two kids, or out on a date night with his wife.

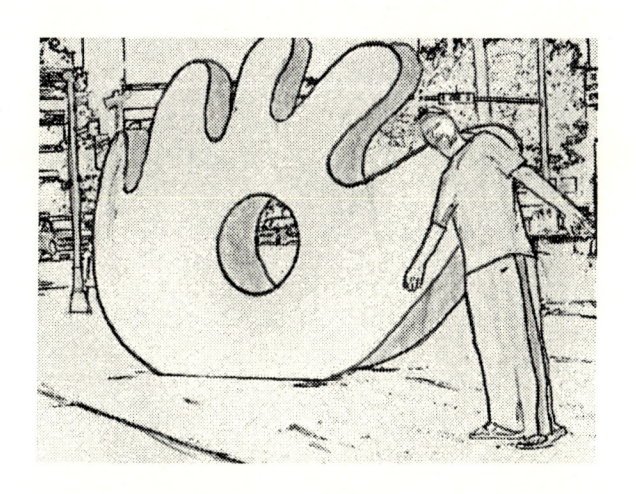

"After grand successes and a few bombs, somewhere along the way I realized the formula for success and invented the *Bore-o-Meter*. Now I can only pass the torch to other dads and hope they enjoy the ride."

–Ean Vent

Acknowledgments

This book wouldn't exist without the unwavering encouragement from my wife. Thanks my love, for trusting me out in the city with your most precious cargo. You said it most eloquently: "Dad Duty does not stop the minute you arrive back home. Dad Duty means doing all the little things that add up to being a great father. Like tying the shoes when everyone is running late, or changing that last load of laundry, or dealing with a diaper blowout. These are the things that give a woman entirely new reasons to love her man." She's right. These are the actions that say: "we are in this together." And know this my dear: "I wouldn't want it any other way."

The object of Dad Duty is not to leave mom out while dad and the kids whoop it up. The goal is to say, "Honey, you need a break to maintain sanity, and the kids and I will be ok out on the town." Even more important is to convey: "We're having fun, but your presence will be missed. You are not a slave to the labors of motherhood. You are the lifeblood that keeps the family glued together. Without your presence, a gaping hole will exist." That is the true meaning of Dad Duty, and thanks to my wife for opening my eyes.

Finally, a big thanks to my editor in chief Dr "Papa" T. Fleming (the father and grandfather to over a dozen offspring) for the nuggets of Seattle wisdom that can only be gained from the trenches. Also special thanks to Marilyn (a.k.a "Mammaw") who perfected Grandma-duty, and to Jerry, Katy, Jon, and Sam (my gorilla marketer) for your support and enthusiasm.

NOTES